After Darkness
Light

After Darkness Light

John Calvin

Catherine Mackenzie

CF4•K

Copyright © 2009 Catherine Mackenzie
Paperback ISBN: 978-1-78191-550-9
epub ISBN: 978-1-84550-893-7
mobi ISBN: 978-1-84550-894-4

Reprinted in 2014, 2016 and 2024

First published in 2009
ISBN: 978-1-84550-084-9

Published by
Christian Focus Publications, Geanies House, Fearn,
Ross-shire, IV20 1TW, Scotland, U.K.
Tel: +44 (0)1862 871011, Fax: +44 (0)1862 871699
www.christianfocus.com
email: info@christianfocus.com

Cover design by Daniel van Straaten
Illustrated by Jeff Anderson
Printed and bound in Denmark by Nørhaven

All rights reserved. No part of this publication may be reproduced, stored in a retrieval system, or transmitted, in any form, by any means, electronic, mechanical, photocopying, recording or otherwise without the prior permission of the publisher or a licence permitting restricted copying. In the U.K. such licences are issued by the Copyright Licensing Agency, 4 Battlebridge Lane, London, SE1 2HX www.cla.co.uk

* * *

With thanks to John van Eyk and Josh van Eyk for their input to this book. Also to Marianne Ross and Irene Howat whose encouragement and direction to my writing over the years are much appreciated.

Contents

Introduction 7
Midnight Rider 9
Memories and Fears 17
Plans and Playmates 25
Tonsure and Travels 33
La Marche and Montaigu 41
From Paris to Orléans 49
And then there was Light 67
Reformer on the Run 81
Basel and Books 91
Geneva – Part One 99
In Need of a Wife 113
Geneva – Part Two 119
Troubles and Trials 135
A College and a Conclusion 143
Bibliography 151
John Calvin Timeline 152
Reformed Theology 154
Thinking Further Topics 156

Introduction

One of the things you realise when you sit down to write a book on John Calvin, is how much material you have available to you. There are many books and articles about the famous Reformer. You then realise how little there is available about his childhood and his conversion, perhaps the two areas of his life that are of most interest to modern day readers.

As regards Calvin's childhood, there are key facts that every biographer agrees with, but there are other things such as dates and the sequence of events that are debated. In this book I have used several books in my research, but I have decided to take all historical dates from *John Calvin: Revolutionary, Theologian, Pastor* by Williston Walker or *John Calvin: A full-scale life of the controversial Reformation leader and influential theologian* by T.H.L. Parker.

For ease of reading and understanding, I have taken some liberties through the use of dialogue. All quotes in italics, are those words actually said or written by Calvin himself. Other dialogue is imagined, but hopefully in such a way that will help readers to understand the background to Calvin's life and the thinking behind the Reformation.

Calvin left very little information about the actual events surrounding his conversion. There are names of various people who influenced his life for good. It is not known if it was his conversations with Pierre that eventually brought him to trust in the Lord Jesus Christ, but it is highly likely that such conversations took place. Pierre was a convinced Reformer, some time before Calvin. They were both in Paris, Orléans and Basel at the same times. Conversations of a religious and spiritual nature must have taken place. Melchior did influence Calvin in similar ways. Both men must have encouraged Calvin to read the Bible as well as Reformed literature.

You might wonder, 'Why celebrate the anniversary of a sixteenth-century theologian?' The answer is simple: our world would be a darker place without the teaching he gave us. Our religious and democratic liberties owe a lot to what John Calvin began through his teachings and life.

After Darkness Light should, however, be read as a summary and introduction to the life of John Calvin. It is not written by an expert, but by someone who was discovering for herself the life of the great Reformer.

I hope that this little book will ignite your interest in the life of one of Europe's great Reformers.

There is a lot to learn and there are many surprises along the way!

Midnight Rider

Thundering hooves clattered along the cobbled streets. The heaving breath of a hard-ridden horse left soft clouds of steam in the rider's wake. The thick black night was broken only by a slight sliver of moon that appeared and then disappeared again. Occasional street torches cast a dull amber light at the corners of chapels and inns as the horse and rider rode on; otherwise the city of Noyon was both dark and silent. The scrape of horse hoof against cobbled stone was the only sign that someone was in a mighty hurry that night. A quick look out of a window by a sleepless householder would not have been fast enough to catch even a glimpse of them. The midnight gallopers vanished through the streets of Noyon as quickly as a fork of distant lightning zigzagged through the sky.

A terse, anxious voice urged the flagging horse on. Small drops of rain were ignored by both mount and rider. Any sign of weariness on the part of the horse was met with a stern flick of the whip. They were on an urgent mission – a matter of life or death.

The further into the city they went, the more cramped and forbidding the streets felt. Buildings sprawled out in all directions. The city walls of Noyon rose high above. They gave necessary protection to the secluded squares and twisting alleyways that made the midnight rider's task so difficult. A town that was well known during the day was a labyrinth of confusion when night-time fell.

'God willing, the patient will still be alive when I arrive,' the young rider muttered to his horse as he searched desperately for some landmark by which to guide him. 'For what good is a doctor if he cannot, at first, find his patient? Cures and medicine are all very well, but they are totally useless sitting inside this satchel of mine,' the doctor chafed inwardly. 'Lord Montmor assured me that the house was in a prosperous commercial area, not far from a chapel. Now what chapel was it?' he asked himself, peering earnestly around the dark streets once again.

Reining his mount in, he tried to find his bearings. The horse's flanks rose and fell under the saddle; glad of a rest, it let its head droop toward the ground in search of a mouthful of grass, or a puddle of fresh rainwater to quench its thirst. But not for long. The doctor urged the horse on again as he anxiously looked one way and then another. 'What was it Lord Montmor said to me before I left? "The patient's name is Gérard Calvin – or at least it's his wife who is sick – he's a notary in the town and the chapel is ..." Ah! That's right – Sainte-Godeberte!'

It wasn't that the name of the chapel had suddenly popped back into his head – the chapel itself had suddenly appeared as his horse turned the corner near the corn market square.

'Now I know that the house is directly across from the church. If I take a moment or two, I'm sure to find it. But I must make haste ... Lord Montmor said that the woman in question is in danger of losing her life. Perhaps he should have sent for the family priest and not the family doctor.' Again the young man urgently looked for some signpost or street name that would give him a clue as to where he was.

'They live in a comfortable house on the Place au Blé, between La Ruelle des Porcelets and Rue Formentière. But which of these streets is the right one?' he anxiously exclaimed. 'I can see the towers of the cathedral on one side and the chapel on the other. I am definitely in the right area!'

The loud thud of a door slamming interrupted the doctor's thoughts. 'What was that?' He turned his horse around and trotted towards where he had heard the sound.

A house halfway down a side street was lit up like a beacon. Lamps were on in several windows. The door opened and shut again, loudly. The occupants weren't worried about waking their neighbours. Perhaps this was the house he had been sent to find?

A servant girl was now running down the street, anxious and out of breath. 'Hey there!' the doctor called out, trying to get the girl's attention. But she would not stop. 'I can't talk to you now, sir. I'm on an urgent errand to fetch the priest. Madame Calvin is at death's door.' And with that the young girl disappeared into the night.

Just then the light of the moon and the dull flame from the dying embers of a street torch, lit up a name at the doctor's shoulder, 'Place au Blé'. With great relief the young man tethered his horse and rushed up to Gérard Calvin's house. He knocked loudly on the door and didn't cease until it had been opened. 'Gérard Calvin, I'm here to see Mr Gérard Calvin on the request of Lord Montmor. I'm his personal physician.'

At that, a hand reached out into the darkness and dragged him into the hallway. 'Quickly now, I beg of you. I've sent for the priest, but if you can do anything we may not need his services tonight. My wife appears to have reached a crisis in her illness; her fever grows ever higher and her breathing ever lower.'

As the anxious husband recounted symptom after symptom on their way to the sick chamber, the doctor quickly began to realise that it wasn't the priest's services that were unneeded, but his own. He was only sorry that he had come. 'It appears that all I am giving this loving husband is false hope,' he thought ruefully.

In fact he had only been in her chamber for twenty minutes at the most when Jeanne Le Franc Calvin breathed her last. The frantic priest had barely managed to utter a prayer over the dying woman, before she closed her eyes in death.

'What good is a priest now?' thought the doctor. 'About as good as a doctor,' he pondered. 'All there is to care for now is a dead body.'

Sighing, he allowed the husband and the out-of-breath priest to begin the process of mourning. Quitting the room, he sat down on a seat in the corridor and buried his head in his hands. Just then, from out of the corner of his eye he caught a glimpse of a white nightshirt, inside it a small child, not much more than three or four years old.

'Who are you?' asked the child.

But before the doctor could answer, the door to the sick-room opened and Mr Calvin stepped out. 'John, fetch your brothers. You can see your mother now.'

The face of the little boy lit up. 'May I take my wooden horse in to show her? She would like to see that, I'm sure – now she's better.'

The doctor sighed as he picked up his satchel. How do you tell a young child that his mother will never look at his toys again? The last he saw of the Calvins, was when three little boys were being ushered into their mother's room. The doctor disappeared, but one little boy turned round and looked puzzled at the quick appearance and disappearance of this strange man.

Young John had woken up that night to the sound of servants rushing to and fro. Doors slammed and feet hammered up and down the corridor. It was a strange thing for the little boy to witness, as for weeks now he had been forbidden to make as much as a sound indoors. As he listened to the anxious calls of servants running up and down the stairs, John was very confused. 'I thought Mother didn't like noise any more and that everyone had to be quiet. Why are they all running around playing games at night? I'm not allowed to do it, even during the day.'

Someone suddenly called out, 'Clear away that linen and get firewood to the sick-room immediately.'

A thought came to young John's mind as he lay snuggled under his blankets. Had he cleared away the carpet bowls as he had been told? he wondered. It was one of his favourite games and he loved to play it in the long corridor outside his bedroom. Today, however, he had been kept to his room all day with only the bowls and his brothers to keep him amused. But, if he hadn't cleared the bowls away, as he had been told, then the maid might not allow him to play with them tomorrow and that wouldn't do at all. John immediately scrunched up his eyes tightly.

Even in the dark he could still see. All he had to do was close his eyes and John could picture in his mind exactly where everything was. A chair was on his right and a small table on his left. The window was at the other end of the room. And yes, he had pushed the carpet bowls under the bed. He remembered now.

In fact he found it very easy to remember things — stories, poems, things that people said; they were all inside his head just waiting to come out again. At that

John Calvin

moment, John's thoughts stopped ... then started again. With all the noise going on, he had forgotten to listen for one sound — the sound of his mother. He had grown so used to her hacking cough over the last few weeks, that now its absence appeared to him to be the loudest sound in the whole house. 'Is she better, now that she has stopped coughing?' he wondered.

The front door slammed and footsteps hurried up the stairs. He could make out his father's voice and the voice of a stranger could be heard also. John pulled away the covers and slipped out of bed. Quietly, he tiptoed to the bedroom door. But he could have stomped his feet all the way; nobody would have paid him the slightest bit of attention.

A maid rushed past, bringing a basin of hot steaming water from the kitchen. The man who helped with the yard and garden work, was struggling up the stairs with more kindling for the fire in his mother's room. Then suddenly the door slammed yet again and a priest ran up the stairs, his gown flapping, a crucifix dangling in a most undignified way from around his neck.

'What is going on?' John wondered as he burrowed down to sit and watch. The priest rushed into his mother's bedroom and moments later John noticed a stranger leaving it. He was looking tired, rather dirty and very sad.

'Who are you?' the little boy asked. But John never discovered who the stranger was. In a few moments his childhood had been changed for ever.

As he was ushered into his mother's room, he soon realised why she didn't want to see his toy horse.

'You can't see anything when you are dead,' his older brother explained to him. 'Mother is dead and we shan't see her again either.'

'Not even if we close our eyes tight and imagine her?' John asked, puzzled.

Over the next few weeks, he would try that. However, what worked for dressers, tables and carpet bowls didn't seem to work for loving mothers who were no longer with you. For a few weeks, he would try to conjure up the colour of her hair and the exact tint of her eyes, but even when he was pretty sure it was an accurate picture, it just didn't feel right, it was never the same. She was in his mind, she was in his heart, but she just wasn't there.

A darkness that little John had not been aware of before had now appeared in his life. Something was missing – his mother, a feeling of peace, a sense that everything was as it was supposed to be. He felt none of these things any more. With this deep sort of darkness all around, he longed for someone to light a candle so that it would be light and joy once again … but no wax candle, however bright, could help little John Calvin.

Memories and Fears

The years passed and all John had were dim memories of his mother, but he cherished them nonetheless. Even though his father had already remarried, John loved to picture his first mother and the fun and games they had had together.

There had been many events and significant moments where he had missed her presence. There had been birthdays which she hadn't been at and so many accomplishments she hadn't witnessed. She hadn't seen him learn to read or ride his first pony, but his father had been there urging him on.

Gérard Calvin had great ambitions for his sons and wanted them to make the most of their education. However, the ambitious father could see that John was the brightest of the three by far. He knew that he would have to make extra special plans for him.

'If I put him in the way of rich and noble men, the connections that he'll make will serve him well,' he schemed. 'John could get a career in the church or maybe the law. For that, he'll need a university education. I'll need to start planning things soon.'

Even as a young lad John Calvin's life was being mapped out for him. His father was thinking of sending him to university at quite a young age. He hadn't even attended his first school and he was being taught lies … lies about important things such as life and death.

And it was thoughts about these deep and important things, that often filled John's head after his mother's death. Thoughts of heaven and hell would interrupt his dreams at night and his thoughts during the day. His deep, dark eyes would appear troubled as he grappled with these weighty matters.

Only wicked people went to hell, those who didn't believe in anything that the Bible said – heathens, pagans and immoral people. Only truly good people went straight to heaven. Everyone else had to spend some time in Purgatory – suffering – in order to make them ready for heaven.

He was sure that his mother wouldn't spend much time in Purgatory. She may not even have had to go there at all. His beautiful, smiling mother, so gentle and kind must be one of those blessed people who went straight to the arms of the Virgin Mary and Jesus.

'But how can I be sure?' he wondered.

In the garden, one afternoon, John was playing with his brothers. They kicked a ball around and then played on a rope swing that hung from a chestnut tree, overlooking the lane. Thoughts of eternity crept into John's heart and he wandered off to find a quiet corner somewhere. He had a half-eaten apple in his pocket. Fishing it out, he took a bite and sat down to think.

John Calvin

John had asked the priest many times about how he could be ready for heaven. Almost every time he got a different answer. There were just so many things you had to accomplish. Now his mother had been a busy woman with many things to do such as cooking meals, mending clothes and other household chores. John was worried that she may have been too busy to prepare herself for dying, because she'd had so much living to do. He shivered at the thought and a tear began to trickle down his slightly freckled cheek.

John tried not to think of it, but he couldn't help himself. The thought of Purgatory sent shivers down his spine. He remembered the solemn face of the priest, when he had told the children about what happened after death. 'Purgatory is where sinners go to after they die; it is where you will be punished for the sins you commit during your life on earth. It is a place of preparation. Without the sufferings you receive in Purgatory you cannot be made fit for heaven.'

'So how do we get out of there?' one anxious little girl asked.

'If you live a good life here on earth then, that will be taken into account. Your good works in this life, the money you pay to the church and other good deeds will all speed your exit from that dreadful place. Your relatives must also pray to the Virgin Mary for you to be released from your torment. They must pay money to the church and light candles. These are the only ways to ensure your release from Purgatory.'

Flicking his straggly brown hair from off his face, John's thoughts came back to the present. A butterfly flitted past, drifting one way and then the next. It was a little thing and would only live for a brief spell. But then John's thoughts began to follow the pattern of the butterfly, first one way and then the other.

'How long will I live? Will I ever be good enough? Will I have to stay in Purgatory for a very long time?'

However, as young John's thoughts flitted to life, then death and then back again, some great and learned men in cathedrals and universities across Europe were thinking about the same things.

They had actually started to question what the Roman Catholic Church taught its followers. These men had studied the Bible for themselves and discovered that there was no such place as Purgatory. Now John had never been allowed to read a Bible, far less own one, so he didn't know that Purgatory didn't exist. Yet the priests taught that it existed, because it was a good source of revenue for them. As long as people were frightened about Purgatory, you would get them to pay good money to be saved from it. The church had become corrupted and was being led by evil men. Reform was required.

But John didn't know anything about Reform or revenues or even very much about the Bible. For now, his young mind was worried about a place that didn't even exist. 'If you want to escape Purgatory, the church says you have to do lots of things,' John thought to himself. He cast his mind back to all those conversations he'd had with the priest.

'Live a good life, John. Obey the Scriptures, your parents, the church.'

'Pray to the Virgin Mary, young man. She will help you. She'll speak to her Son, the Lord Jesus, on your behalf, because you are simply too sinful to speak to him on your own. You need Mary to be on your side.'

'Don't forget to pray to the saints. There are many saints who will listen to your prayers in order to help you.'

'Always give money to the church. God, the Virgin Mary and the saints will be pleased with you, John, if you give as much money as you can. Generous men and women will certainly escape the fires of Purgatory.'

'Light candles at the cathedral, for when you light a candle in the name of a dead relative, you will reduce their time in Purgatory and they will get to heaven all the quicker.'

'Confess your sins to the priest. He will absolve you from them and forgive you.'

'Any time you sin, pay some money to the church as penance.'

'Go on a pilgrimage whenever you can and don't forget to pay the monks and friars when you get there.'

John sighed. Perhaps he would light a candle for his mother, the next time he was at the cathedral. There was a statue of the Virgin Mary there. He would stand in front of it and pray. He could ask the Holy Virgin to release his mother from Purgatory. He'd pray to a few of the other saints too, whose images were hanging on the walls or in alcoves around the church building.

He went to confession regularly now. It was part of his life and he was quite used to it. In a private little corner, the priest would listen to you, as you told him about all the misdemeanours you had done since the last time you had come to confess your sins. Then he would absolve you or forgive you for them.

You could also pay money to the priests if you had it and they would arrange for your sins to be forgiven. That was called paying penance.

As John had the last bite of his apple, he gave a big sigh. It didn't matter how many good things you did to get into heaven, you always did more bad things that would keep you out. So you had to do more good things to help you get in, but then you'd do more bad things. So you had to do more good things. Yes, it was your sins that made God angry with you and kept you out of heaven. 'If only I could stop doing them,' John exclaimed to himself. 'That would be a huge help. But every time I go to confession I seem to have a long list of new sins for the priest to absolve.'

Each new day brought fresh sin and new trouble. One day, he would steal a piece of apple from a plate in the kitchen, on the next he would fight with his brothers over some toy or other. If he fought with Charles, his older brother, he often lost, but when he fought with Antoine, the youngest, he often won. But whether he won or lost, fighting was a sin and he would have to go to confession to get his sins forgiven.

Just then, John remembered that he and his mother had once gone on a pilgrimage. 'Surely that must be a good thing,' thought John. It hadn't been a very long pilgrimage, but a pilgrimage didn't have to be to a very far place. The abbey at Ourscamp was, in fact, only four miles away from the town of Noyon. His mother had felt the need to visit the abbey to pray. She had brought her young son with her for company.

Now, some abbeys boasted that they possessed the finger of a disciple; others claimed they had a relic or two from the Last Supper; many cathedrals said that they actually possessed a piece of wood from the cross that Jesus Christ was crucified on. So, people from far and near would make special visits to these places, in order to see the relics and pray to them.

The Notre-Dame d'Ourscamp Abbey had quite a grizzly relic, the skull of St. Anne. John remembered that at one point during their visit, his mother had made him kiss it. He grimaced at the memory, but brightened at the thought that his mother had been on a pilgrimage. It was one of those things that the priests said got you into heaven.

'Well,' thought John, 'perhaps Mother won't be in Purgatory since she has been on a pilgrimage.'

It was a little piece of hope for John to grasp at. But as stalks of grass will not save a man who is falling over a cliff, so the lies that John was taught would not save his or anyone else's soul from death.

Just then, John noticed that his brothers were being ushered back into the house. A maid called out to him, 'Come on, Master John. Don't dilly-dally. Lord Montmor is coming to visit with your father. You boys are to clean yourselves up and wait in the parlour when they arrive. Hurry up now, your brothers are already on their way upstairs.'

John looked puzzled. He had heard of Lord Montmor before and knew of his importance. The name of Montmor was one of the noblest names in the town of Noyon and belonged to a very wealthy family. But the thought of having to clean his face twice in one day did not give young John any joy at all. He had cleaned it after breakfast; surely that was enough for anybody! However, there was no way out. Father's word was law and you never argued with the maid. Dusting down his breeches, John picked himself up and ran back into the house.

Plans and Playmates

With clean clothes on, scrubbed faces and hair all in place, the three Calvin boys were soon presentable and sent down to the parlour. The new Mrs Calvin gave the boys strict instructions to behave themselves before she reached for the parlour door and pushed it open.

John sighed at the thought of an afternoon spent with adults for company, but as he entered the parlour his face brightened. His father's visitors also included two young boys. Maybe this visit wouldn't be as boring as he had feared.

'Come in, come in,' John's father urged. 'Lord Montmor, let me introduce my wife and my sons Charles, John and Antoine. Boys, this is Lord Montmor and his sons Joachim and Ives.'

John bowed politely and sat down on a bench beside the fireplace. Mrs Calvin was not in the room long, before she made her apologies. A wailing infant was calling from the back of the house. John's new little sister was obviously causing trouble for the maids.

John wished he were in the kitchen with baby Marie — at least there he wouldn't have to sit still so much. But then he cast a glance at the other two lads across the room. One smiled pleasantly, while the other stuck out his tongue and crossed his eyes. John found it very hard not to burst out laughing. Eventually their fathers both took pity on them.

'Charles, John, Antoine – why don't you take your guests for a walk outside? You could go as far as the river and back. Lord Montmor and I have much to discuss. I am sure you boys would prefer to be outside on such a fine afternoon as this.'

Antoine immediately jumped to his feet. Charles and John politely bowed and then all five boys ran outside for fresh air and exercise. Joachim, the cross-eyed mischief, yelled out as they escaped into the back lane. 'Race you to the bridge; last one there's a wonky-donkey!' And with that all the boys took to their heels.

Alone in the parlour, the two men began the discussion they had been planning.

'I see your boys are bright, healthy young lads,' Lord Montmor observed.

'They are,' Gérard agreed. 'John, however, is the cleverest. Charles does well enough, but there is something about John. He has a clear mind and remembers everything. I am making plans for his future. I can see him in the church or maybe the law.'

'Good man, Gérard,' Lord Montmor agreed. 'You need to plan ahead. If you want an ecclesiastical or legal career for John you'll have to start thinking

John Calvin

about university. I'm certain that your son is more than capable.

'From our brief meeting, I can see that he has a good manner. Quiet, but not sullen. He should do well. If you are right and he proves to be as bright as you suspect, you'll want him to go far.'

'We will send John to *The Capettes* after the summer. Charles has already begun his studies there,' Gérard pointed out.

'*The Capettes* is a good school,' Lord Montmor affirmed, 'especially if you are considering a career in the church. But I have a plan that might help him on to even greater things.'

'What do you mean?' Mr Calvin enquired.

'What I mean is this. The Hangest family tutor their boys, as do we. The tutors we choose are men taken from the best universities and over time their influence on John's education could be considerable.

'The Hangests, as you know, are related to the Bishop – and Adrien de Hangest and I would be willing to have your son attend tutorials at our homes.

'If John were to have the benefits of personal tutors, as well as the advantages of more noble society, then who knows how high he could climb?'

'You are most generous, Lord Montmor. You are showing us great ...'

Lord Montmor interrupted his host with a short wave of the hand. 'Say nothing of it, nothing at all. Your John is gifted. We are all agreed about that. It would be a great shame to see those gifts wasted. Let's both do our best to make sure that at least one of your sons excels in the world.

'The church is certainly the place for a young man to make a name for himself these days. Let's just hope that he avoids the Lutheran heresy. It seems to be making headway even amongst some of our more illustrious academics.'

'Surely not!' Gérard Calvin exclaimed. 'It's just a flash in the pan, as they say. One discontented monk who nailed a list of complaints to a cathedral door in Wittenburg a few years ago. That Martin Luther is a thorn in the side of the church, but he'll be rooted out easily enough.'

'Don't assume anything, Gérard,' Lord Montmor declared. 'These heresies even make their way into France. Switzerland is under the preaching of one named Zwingli who is of the 'Reformation' persuasion. It seems that every country in northern Europe has been infected by this doctrine of Reform. Why, there are Lutherans in Noyon. You can't escape them even in our city.

'These men declare that the Holy Roman Church does not teach the truth. They say that the priests care more about the money in their pockets than teaching the Bible. They would have the man in the street read God's Word for himself and be placed under the authority of it and his own conscience ... rather than under the authority of His Holiness the Pope.'

'That sounds like revolutionary talk to me,' Gérard tutted. 'It is only the church that can give the right direction to a man's conscience. We can't have people reading the Bible willy-nilly like that. Who knows what would happen then?'

'Quite right! That's why it's dangerous and we should do our best to destroy it at its core. We must get our best minds in the church to fight against those Reformation lies.'

Gérard nodded his head in agreement. He didn't always see eye to eye with everything the church said, but to have ordinary people reading the Bible in their own language, without any leadership from priest or pope, was a recipe for disaster. It didn't bear thinking of!

Instead Gérard congratulated himself on having such an intelligent son who was sure to avoid these Reforming heresies. 'He's far too wise to get himself embroiled in all that,' he muttered to himself.

Over the next few months, both John and Charles enjoyed the friendship of the Montmor boys and Claude de Hangest, Adrien de Hangest's son. But it was John they favoured most, it was John who attended tutorials and even lived in their homes during the holidays.

One morning, towards the end of the long summer vacation John, Charles and Antoine met up with the Montmor boys and Claude in order to go on a hike along the banks of the River Verse. A picnic had been packed. So with walking sticks and backpacks they set off on their adventure.

The cathedral bells rang in the distance, calling the faithful of Noyon to yet another Mass or service. As the pealing bells died down the young boys arrived at a large chestnut tree, then unpacked their picnic and got stuck in. 'The chestnuts aren't ready,' John sighed, 'but by the time I go to school there will be plenty.'

Joachim nodded while munching away on a large chunk of bread and cheese. 'You're going to the Collège des Capettes, aren't you, John?'

'Yes. I'm looking forward to it. I'll still be coming to some of your tutorials though.'

Joachim laughed, 'More fool you. You wouldn't catch me going to school and getting tutorials from Old Stodgy Face.'

All the boys laughed at Joachim's nickname for the dull tutor.

Joachim continued, 'I'm sure you'll have loads more fun at school. The sons of the nobility aren't sent to ordinary schools. I wish we could go.'

Charles sneered. 'Don't be so sure. The masters at *The Capettes* can be very strict, harsh sometimes. They'll beat a boy who doesn't learn his lessons.'

John shivered slightly at the thought. 'I suppose that means that they all learn their lessons very, very well,' he muttered.

'You'd think they would,' Charles agreed. 'But it's not always the case. I'm sure you'll do fine, John – we all know how clever you are. However, not all boys are as gifted as you. I've had the strap several times for getting my Latin grammar mixed up.'

'The strap is no hardship,' Joachim laughed. 'I get strapped all the time at home. I'm always getting into some mischief or other.'

Charles nodded. 'I'm sure you are. But bear in mind you haven't felt a Capettes strap, that's all I can say. My masters beat me far harder than father does.'

Joachim and Ives looked slightly relieved. Perhaps tutoring at home wasn't such a bad thing after all.

Soon the thoughts and worries about schools and tutors were put to one side and all the boys enjoyed a day's hike along the river, chasing squirrels, skimming stones and searching for the best places to fish from. As the sun slowly started to descend behind the high woods, the exhausted boys began to make their way back along the River Verse. Once they had returned to the Place au Blé and their friends had left for home, Mrs Calvin mentioned that Mr Calvin wished to see John in his study.

Tonsure and Travels

Warm from his day in the outdoors, and refreshed from a long cool drink, John ran up the stairs two at a time. He was soon knocking at the study door.

'Come in John,' replied his father. 'I have some important information to discuss with you.'

John entered and, taking a seat beside his father, he waited to hear what he had to say.

'I've heard good reports from Lord Montmor and the tutor he employs. If you do well at *The Capettes,* I am convinced that one day you will study at the university.'

It would be a grand thing to be sent to university. But could they afford it? John wondered.

Gérard Calvin paced up and down the room. 'Because you are now moving in nobler circles than other boys your age, you have been given privileges your older brother, Charles, has not been blessed with. Our close acquaintance with Lord Montmor and the Hangests is a magnificent honour. In fact, some time ago, Bishop Hangest himself was influential in advancing our family fortunes immensely.

'It is through our connections with him, that we obtained the chaplaincy at the altar of La Gésine in the cathedral. This means that I can personally finance your university education. It has given me enough money to put Charles through college too.

'The altar of La Gésine is profitable. Hopefully, over time we will purchase other chaplaincies like this and improve our position in the world.'

John's puzzled face did not remain unnoticed by his father.

'What is worrying you, son?' he asked.

'I'm not worried, father, it's just that … will Charles or I need to preach or do services?'

'Not at all,' his father laughed. 'Think about it like a business arrangement. We pay the church money and every time someone places money at the altar of La Gésine, then we receive some of the donation. I will pay a priest a small salary to say prayers and do the other duties. All you have to do is shave off the hair on the top of your head like Charles.'

John sighed; he'd forgotten about that. A year or so ago, Charles had received the tonsure. This was the name given to the hairstyle that was the sign that you belonged to a clerical order.

He remembered when Charles had had his hair shaved off. John had laughed at the sight and then felt the sting of his father's strap for his cheek. Just then, a snigger escaped from John without his knowledge.

'This is not funny, John!' his father barked sternly.

John stifled his giggles. The funny hairstyle would be on his head next. That soon made him sober up.

John Calvin

Mrs Calvin arrived in the study with a bowl of warm water and a razor. In no time at all, John had a completely smooth crown – and just a circle of hair around his forehead and ears. A pile of straggly brown locks lay in clumps at his feet.

Afterwards, he sheepishly made his way back into the kitchen and young Antoine laughed out loud.

Mrs Calvin turned to John and said, 'Don't worry, his time will come. It will feel strange for a while, but you'll soon get used to it. Just remember, the tonsure shows that you hold office in the church. That is a great thing.'

John sighed and nodded. Mrs Calvin pulled out a pastry from the pantry and gave it to John, who smiled as he bit into it, crumbs falling everywhere as he munched.

The years flew by and John's appetite for learning grew even greater than his appetite for food at times. *The Capettes* schooling and the tutorials were challenging him, but probably not enough. He was still sailing through his lessons with almost perfect ease.

Joachim, Ives and Claude still went on hikes and hunting trips with Charles and John, but they had less and less time to devote to pleasure. Their tutor made sure of that. They had to focus on their futures and that meant studying!

Gone were the boys who could spend their afternoons fishing and chasing squirrels. John began to realise that Noyon would not always be his home. He began to wonder what it would be like to live away from friends and family, in a big city that he had never seen before. But whenever John started worrying about things like that, he would reassure himself with the thought that all those changes were a long way off. He didn't have to worry about university just yet.

Or at least that was what John thought.

There came an evening, when Lord Montmor and Adrien de Hangest paid a visit. They had brought with them the Montmors' tutor so Gérard Calvin knew that they must be here to discuss John's future. Gérard invited the gentlemen up to his study, where they would have more privacy.

'At thirteen years of age, is John ready for university?' Gérard asked. He was astonished to hear that the noble lords and the tutor were thinking he should send John to university this year, instead of next. 'Do you think it's the right time for him to go?'

'I believe so,' replied the tutor. 'He shows great promise and he is nearly fourteen years old. Many students start their university careers at that age. In fact, Lord Montmor's boys and Claude de Hangest will attend Paris University at the start of the new term. I would recommend that you send John also.'

Gérard quietly nodded his head. It was probably a wise decision to send John away from Noyon, simply for his own safety. Fresh cases of the plague arose daily. The sight of corpses being trundled through the streets on carts was commonplace now.

Gérard scratched his head and did some quick calculations. He had planned well, saved some money and invested what he could. The chaplaincy profits meant that sending John to university this summer rather than next, was not only possible, but a very good idea.

'Very well then,' Gérard agreed. 'John shall accompany your sons to Paris.' Turning to Lord Montmor he asked, 'What plans have you made?'

Lord Montmor stretched back in his chair. 'We will be sending the tutor with the boys as far as the capital. Even though they assume that they are adults now, they'll need some supervision on the journey,' he explained. 'He'll also stay with them in Paris for some time after that, to give my sons extra tutorials in addition to their university lessons. Joachim at least will need some additional help.'

'We have accommodation organised for all three,' Hangest interrupted. 'We could easily give John a place too. Both Montmor and I would be more than glad to see John boarding with our boys. He could be a good influence, I believe,' Hangest chuckled.

Gérard knew that it was a great offer, but his pride didn't allow him to become beholden to the noble lords. They had done enough for John already.

'Thank you,' Gérard declared. 'However, my brother Richard is a Paris locksmith who lives near the Church of Saint-Germain l'Auxerrois. John will live with him.

'But it is a good idea that they travel together. It will offer them some protection from highwaymen and such like. If they leave soon they will also escape this awful plague that is cursing our town.'

'My thoughts exactly,' agreed Montmor as he rose to leave. 'So it's agreed. We'll set the wheels in motion and before the end of the summer the boys will begin their journey to Paris.'

Gérard Calvin accompanied his guests to the door. As they were leaving he added, 'Give me a couple of weeks to get the finances in place. I'll need to contact the university too as well as the boy's uncle, but before too long all should be ready.'

And it was. In a matter of weeks the boys were gathering their possessions in order to travel to Europe's greatest seat of learning. When the morning came for his departure it was an excited, but apprehensive John that said goodbye to his family.

Mrs Calvin clutched protectively at another baby sister who might be fully grown by the time John returned to Noyon, if he ever did.

Antoine waved enthusiastically as John mounted his horse. Looking at his younger brother cheered John out of his sombre frame of mind. Antoine's tonsure was a very amusing sight from the height of his mount. It only seemed like yesterday that John had been getting his head shaved for the first time.

Now Antoine had the same style, and a couple of little sisters to laugh at him.

Just then Gérard Calvin spoke one last piece of advice to his son before he left.

'You will now mix in different circles, John, and will seldom return to the town of your birth. You have been tutored with the sons of noblemen and aristocrats, you have befriended sons of bishops and lords, you will now be trained by some of the greatest minds that this country has to offer. But do not forget us, John. Do not forget your family or your origins.

'You are the offspring of common people, do not forget that. But now you are at home with the greatest nobility of the land. You may eat at their tables without blushing.

'We have great hopes for you, John. May God go with you.' He called the last lines out as the tutor began to turn his horse around and lead the small group of students onto the open road.

It was a road that would take them far away from Noyon to the capital city they so longed to see. It was a road that would take them away from their childhood to a new future.

John turned round in his saddle as they made their way through the corn market square. His father stood with a hand raised. John waved in farewell once more. Then they lost sight of each other and the party of young scholars began to make their way towards the city gates.

The journey would involve some overnight stops, an adventure for John who hadn't ventured more than five miles beyond the city walls of Noyon. As the young men rode joyfully along, Joachim turned to smile at his fellow riders. 'This is the beginning of the rest of our lives,' he declared boldly. 'It is the year 1523 and we are in the middle of a wonderful modern age. I wonder what magnificent things we shall do.'

Ives imagined that he would be a great lawyer with plenty of riches. Joachim rather fancied himself as a daring adventurer before he would settle down to running his father's large estates.

'Claude will be a famous writer. He's so wise and intelligent. Who knows what John here will do? He's got more brains than all of us put together,' Joachim laughed out loud. 'But I am not discouraged; I wasn't made for books and study like Calvin here; I was made for honour and battles. What do you say?' he exclaimed to his companions. 'We shall be victorious! We shall have adventures! Let's hope they're breathtakingly exciting.'

The tutor turned round in his saddle to glare at his energetic charges. 'I have no care for adventures,' he grumbled, 'breathtakingly exciting or otherwise. Let's just get to Paris with our skins intact and our purses unmolested,' he sighed. The stolid little man did not seem to be half as excited about the journey as his students were.

La Marche and Montaigu

The stolid little man wasn't excited about anything that happened en route to Paris. The inns were too hot, the food was too cold. The horses were skittish and the saddles chafed his legs.

The boys, however, thought the inns were splendid places full of what they imagined to be exciting characters and intrigue. The food was the most delicious they'd ever eaten and the days in the saddle the best they'd ever spent.

Joachim was sure they would come across a highwayman or two on their travels. His tutor fervently prayed that they wouldn't.

Their arrival in the capital was the one thing, however, that took everyone's breath away. Even Joachim was stuck for words and the tutor absent of complaint. Probably, for the first time in his life, John was on a level playing field with his aristocratic friends; none of the boys had ever been in such a heaving metropolis.

'How big is this place?' Claude asked, his neck craning to catch a glimpse of the high buildings.

'How many live here?' Ives wondered as he stared around him at the teeming masses of people.

After Darkness Light

'How will I ever find my uncle in all this?' John gasped as he suddenly realised that his friends would be leaving him to find his own way in one of the largest cities in Europe.

However, a kind stall owner eventually pointed John in the right direction.

With a last wave to his companions Calvin strode off to his new home where a warm welcome and some rather excited relatives were waiting for him.

'So tell me, John,' his uncle asked later that night. 'What are your plans?'

'As far as I can see,' John replied, 'I have a long road ahead of me. First of all I have to go through some sort of preparation course.'

His uncle nodded. 'Hmm. I have heard of that. It's called "the grammar course", I believe. What will they be teaching you in that?'

'Well, I've done the first stage already,' John replied, 'but there are two more stages I've yet to complete. I learned the basics of Latin at the college in Noyon. What I've yet to learn are the more complicated rules of the language and then I'll go on to logic. I've been told to expect a lot of memory work. But it is all to prepare me for doing the Arts Course.'

'Ah yes,' Richard nodded, 'You'll need a good grasp of Latin before you do that.'

'That's correct, Uncle Richard,' John nodded. 'The Collège de la Marche has a good reputation for Latin, particularly in the senior years. Mathurin Cordier teaches there, you know.'

John's uncle and aunt looked at him blankly. 'Mathurin Cordier; I've not heard of him. He can't buy his locks here, then,' John's uncle smiled.

John returned the smile. 'Of course, he won't be my lecturer until I'm in the senior year. But it will be something to look forward to – being taught by one of the greatest Latin scholars in the whole of France.'

John's uncle continued with his questioning. 'What will you do after that?'

'Father has long been planning that I do a degree in theology,' John replied.

'That is a good choice of career for a young man with intelligence,' Richard Calvin acknowledged. 'My, your father must be proud of you. My, my! What a step up in the world to be the first member of the Calvin family to attend university. If I'm not mistaken great times are ahead for you and your family.'

That night John lay in his bed and sighed. It was a strange house and a strange room. He was thankful for the warm welcome of his relatives, but it sounded as though they too had high expectations of him.

It was difficult to have people hoping for so much from you. What if he failed? What if Paris were not the right place for him at all?

For a moment, as the moon hid behind a cloud and the darkness was sucked into every corner of his room, John was sure that he never should have left

Noyon. Quickly, he buried himself under the covers. Tomorrow, he would ask his aunt to supply him with extra candles. He would need them if he were going to study in the evenings. But it would also be good to have a little bit more light, particularly on these dark moonless nights when the stars hardly ever shone.

'I can't even close my eyes and picture this room,' he sighed. 'Everything is so unfamiliar.'

Under the covers, John's whispers gradually faded away as the moon came out again from behind a cloud. The soft silver light calmed his anxiety and soon all that could be heard was gentle snoring.

The first few weeks of study passed in a blur. But despite their hectic activity John, Claude, Joachim and Ives would all find an hour or two to get together and discuss their lessons. All of the lads had different perspectives on their university, but all of them had one thing in common — they were not as good at Latin as they'd thought they were. Even the presence of Old Stodgy, the tutor, had not helped John to get beyond the fourth class.

'The fourth class!' exclaimed Joachim. 'I would have thought that John here would have been higher than that, but no. None of us, it seems, are any good at Latin.'

'Is your father very disappointed?' John smiled.

'What do you think? He paid all that money for a tutor. He, at least, expected me to get into the same class as you. But Father forgets how brainy you are — and how stupid I am,' Joachim sighed.

'Well, I'm not that concerned about my placement. As it turns out class four is a very good one for me.'

'How so?' Ives asked.

'Have you heard of Mathurin Cordier?' John asked, trying to keep his excitement in check.

Ives thought for a moment. 'The name rings a bell. Isn't he a teacher in one of the senior classes?'

'He was,' John explained, eager to let his good news out, 'but he got so fed up of the poor calibre of the lower classes that he decided to teach them himself in order to sort out the problem.

'It just so happens he is taking class four, so I am getting taught by one of the best Latin scholars in the country. He truly is a great teacher, not a bully like the others. He really makes you want to learn.'

Joachim was surprised at the thought of getting on well with a teacher. 'So he's not like Old Stodgy?'

'No, quite different,' John agreed. 'Speaking of which — is Stodgy still around?'

'Of course!' Joachim exclaimed. 'There is certainly no danger of us being left to do whatever we like. When we're not in our classes, that tutor has us bent over our books at every opportunity. The only reason we're talking to you just now, is that the interfering old so-and-so always has a snooze after his dinner. But I shouldn't complain about him too much; the rest of the professors are even worse!'

John laughed as his friend continued to ramble on about his ever growing collection of grouchy tutors and lecturers. He was just glad that he was studying under Cordier. It really was a good start for his university career.

As the weeks passed Calvin found himself enjoying Paris. For many of the other students Paris was a city of pleasure. There were halls of entertainment where shows and dancing drew the crowds. However, John didn't care for that side of the city. Instead he warmed to his studies and the close friendships that he made. John got on so well with his lessons that he was soon promoted from the junior classes. He was sorry to leave Cordier's teaching, but it wasn't that long before he would leave La Marche college for good.

'What did you say, John?' his uncle asked incredulously. 'You're changing college?'

'It appears so. I'm no longer to study at La Marche. I'm to go to Montaigu.'

His uncle and aunt seemed surprised. John had been too at first.

'Why have you made that decision…or was it made for you?' his uncle continued.

'It has been made for me. Father says that I've done so well in my studies, I'm ready to take the Arts Course now. In his letter,' John waved the piece of paper in his hand as he spoke, 'he says that the church in Noyon believes it to be a good decision too. Old Stodgy... I mean Lord Montmor's tutor ... he's really keen. So I suppose I should be happy. The college has a good reputation. It's just that so many people are making decisions for me and I've only been a year or so at La Marche. I'll be sorry to leave.'

Uncle Richard sighed. 'Ah well, John, these things happen, you know – and often they are for the best.'

'I'll also be sorry to leave your home, Uncle,' John added.

'Leave our home?' he exclaimed. 'Surely you don't have to do that, Nephew?'

'I'm afraid I will,' John explained. 'When I go to Montaigu I'll have to move nearer the college. Some students even have to live in – though I hope to avoid that. I might be able to board in a nearby house. It won't be the same, though.'

His aunt nodded, 'That is true. I've heard that Montaigu has a very strict régime. Every moment of your day will be accounted for, every morsel of your food. But it's not a prison, remember that – you'll have some free time, I hope, to come and visit us.'

John smiled. He wasn't so sure about that. His uncle and aunt had no idea about the amount of work that was involved in studying for an Arts degree. John was certain that his spare time would become far less frequent in the coming months. 'I'll try and visit you, Aunt, if my studies allow.'

'Ah well, just make sure that you do,' she admonished him. 'If you're not careful we'll be calling you Midnight Oil like your cousin from Noyon.'

John laughed at that. 'How is Pierre?' he asked.

'Oh, doing well; he's passed all his exams this year. He's always reading some book or other.'

'I would like to meet up with him again. It would be good to catch up and hear his news from Noyon. He is a relative after all, but I feel as though I hardly know him.'

John's aunt then suggested that her husband went to call on Pierre to ask him to dinner.

'Would Saturday be a good day for you, John?' his aunt enquired.

'Thank you, I would enjoy that,' John smiled.

'Very well then,' she replied. 'Your uncle will invite Pierre and we'll have a nice family meal together before you leave for the new college. But I'll tell Pierre and you, John – the usual rules will apply – no books at the table! You can talk about them, but I'll not be blamed for soup and stew stains on vellum and parchment!'

John laughed to himself as he retired to his bedroom that night, 'It sounds as though Pierre and I have a lot in common.'

It turned out that they did. Pierre came up with one or two surprises for his relatives during the meal.

From Paris to Orléans

'What do you mean, you're for Martin Luther?' Uncle Richard exclaimed.

The young earnest Pierre turned to his host and swallowed. 'What I mean is that I've read his writings and have listened to other Reformers. I believe that much of what they are saying is good sense. Not only that, I believe it to be biblical.'

John looked surprised. 'How can you when it is forbidden to own Luther's books or even read them? You are breaking the law, Cousin.'

Pierre sighed. 'I know that, John, and believe me I struggled with that at first. The only reason I am telling you this is that I trust my family...'

Uncle Richard got up from the table to fetch another pitcher of ale. 'You should be more careful, young Pierre. There have been others who have trusted their families before and been the worse for it. But your secret is safe with us, isn't it, John?'

John nodded solemnly. He just couldn't believe that a relative, only two or three years older than he, was a Reformer.

'Surely you can't think it wise that every man is able to read God's Word in his own language. Isn't it

49

the responsibility of the church to control the reading of God's Word to be in command of its teaching?' John's aunt asked.

Pierre took a deep breath, 'The way I see it and others as well, is that the church for many years has been responsible for teaching errors. For example, the teaching of Purgatory is unbiblical. It is simply a way of filling the coffers in Rome and keeping the élite of the church in rich clothing.'

John Calvin looked shocked. To hear his cousin say that Purgatory didn't exist was incredible to his ears.

'You look shocked, Cousin,' Pierre admitted. 'So was I when I first heard this truth. But believe me, if you study the Scriptures for yourself, you will find that Purgatory is nowhere mentioned. It is a fiction of imagination, an invention by popes and cardinals.

'The money that poor people spend to release their loved ones from "torment" finds its way to Rome where it is used to build grander cathedrals, more luxurious palaces. St. Peter's in Rome is being built on the blood, sweat and tears of seamstresses and farmyard labourers. They scrimp and save in order to release their loved ones from the flames of Purgatory and that money goes to bolster up the egos of the Roman Catholic popes and clergy.

'Besides, no sum of money, however large, could ever determine the eternal prospects of any sinner. Indeed, I believe that if the mass populace were able to read Scripture for themselves, they would discover

John Calvin

how many lies their priests told them and throw them all out of the churches forthwith.'

'You speak dangerous heresy, Cousin,' John Calvin exclaimed. 'The college that I am going to expressly forbids any use or even possession of the Bible for individuals.'

'But you are students of theology,' Pierre gasped. 'Don't you see how ridiculous that is, John? You aren't allowed to read the Bible for yourselves, yet you are supposed to be studying the God who wrote it?'

'We will have portions of it read to us at meal times.'

'Yes, portions, but until you study the Bible in its entirety and not just those parts that your teachers think are safe, you will never truly know the Word of God.'

'What do you mean by that?' John demanded. 'Surely the church and the priests teach us what we need to know of the Word of God.'

Pierre thought silently for a moment. 'The next time you go to confession, John, think about this: When do you say the name of Jesus Christ? Is he mentioned at all? Think about what he had to go through to save his people from their sins …' Pierre stopped mid-sentence. His audience looked at him, confused. 'I don't know if I can explain this as well as I should; I just long for you to read the Bible for yourselves!'

For some moments after that everyone ate their meal without saying anything. John's aunt looked across the table at Pierre with a dumbfounded expression on her face.

To break the awkward silence Uncle Richard addressed Pierre once more. 'Well, young man,' he exclaimed. 'Though I am not sure of your beliefs, as you describe them, I do hear that there are more and more of your persuasion in our ever changing world. There are even men and women in our country who are coming to the Reformed faith. Germany is full of them, they say. But hear this, Pierre,' Richard warned. 'There have been people burned in Paris for being Reformed like you, so I beg you to be careful.'

John nodded his head in agreement. Though a firm believer in the Roman Catholic Church, he would not for a moment see his eager young cousin suffer a martyr's death for this cause.

But as he waved farewell to his relative at the doorway, his thoughts wandered back to the discussion they had had of Purgatory.

'How does Pierre believe we are made ready for eternal life, if not through the suffering of Purgatory?' he asked himself. 'Surely there can be no other way to get right with our God ... someone has to suffer for sin. Does he expect that he can get to heaven for free?' John shook his head at the very idea. 'What exactly does he mean about Jesus Christ and what he went through? Is he talking about the crucifixion? If he is, then what does it all mean?' John dismissed the questions from his mind with a shake of the head.

John Calvin

'Those Reformers have no idea what they are doing,' he muttered, before closing the door and heading to his bed.

However, as he lay there in the moonlight he tossed and turned throughout the night. Never, since his years as a young child in Noyon, had his mind been so taken up with thoughts of life and death, the fear of an ever present darkness and a longing for the light. The soft silver beams of a Paris moon, couldn't soothe his anxious thoughts and questions. He shook his head, stuck his hand in a drawer and drew out another candle.

As always, it would be John's studies that would help him to cope with his midnight fears.

A candle burning throughout the night had been a common sight at the locksmith's – it soon became a well-known sight at the Montaigu College too. While most of the other students were in their beds and fast asleep, John would sit at his desk to peer over his notes, books piled high by his elbow. The long black cape and cowl, the uniform of the college, would cover him from head to toe, but it wasn't particularly warm.

Some evenings, he would long for a bowl of his aunt's hearty stew, but poultry and meat and other good things were banned at the college. At best, the soup served from the Montaigu kitchen was weak and tasteless. Nevertheless, John didn't let it put him off his studies. In fact, he sometimes felt that the meagre food sharpened his mind for reading late into the night, so John began to eat a basic diet on purpose. Deliberately, he would go for hours without eating anything, so that he could focus on his readings and meditations.

When his aunt heard of it, she shook her head in disgust. 'If he goes on like that, he'll ruin his innards!' she exclaimed.

Others, who heard of his new diet, also thought it wasn't a good idea. One evening, as John met up with his friends, Ives commented on how John looked a little pale.

'Well,' Joachim exclaimed. 'No wonder – it's that new diet of his. But John, if you're deliberately eating less in order to study more, it's a good job you're at Montaigu – they have hardly any food and more than enough grumpy professors to keep even you happy.'

'It sounds grim,' Ives muttered. 'Even if you were eating all the food they were willing to give you, you'd only be allowed to eat as much bread as you wanted and one thirtieth of a pound of butter or some boiled fruit for your main meal! Don't you get any meat?'

'Can you call herring meat?' John puzzled. 'We sometimes get an egg with vegetables. Theology students get a whole herring or two eggs.'

'Well, that's something,' Joachim laughed. 'Two whole eggs!'

John shrugged his shoulders, 'At least I'm not one of the pauvres[1].'

---

1. French for 'poor'.

'One of the what?' Joachim asked.

'The pauvres,' John repeated. 'The college is divided into three sections depending on what money you have. There are the pensionnaires at the top – they eat together at special tables. They don't mix with the other students. If you're a caméristes like me, then you get to stay in one of the nearby houses at your own expense. If you're a pauvre, you have to live in the college.'

'Is living in the college that bad?' Claude de Hangest enquired.

'Well, if you're a caméristes or a pensionnaire living outside the college then you're allowed to get rid of your own lice and fleas, but if you're a pauvre you have to undergo public checks for the little vermin. I imagine that would be quite humiliating,' John grimaced.

Joachim burst out laughing. 'So living out of college means you avoid the official flea hunt – are there any other perks?'

'Not really, although paying students do get a bit more freedom. Other than that, we have the same schedule as all the other students.

'We have to get up at four in the morning for church and then we attend lectures until six. After that, it's the Mass and then breakfast. From eight until ten we have debates. Our meal is served at eleven, which is followed by prayers and notices. At twelve, the students are questioned about their morning's work and after that for an hour we have a rest period, but during that rest period we have to listen to someone reading. Finally, we get an hour of free time until the afternoon class which finishes at five.'

'That's a long day!' Joachim exclaimed.

'Wait a minute, it's not over yet,' John added. 'We have another church service, which is followed by a discussion on our afternoon lesson. Between our supper and bedtime at eight, there is further time for questions and discussion. Two days a week, we get some time for recreation.'

'What does that involve?' Claude asked.

'We can go for a walk,' John replied.

Joachim and Ives looked at each other. 'Studying in the comfort of your own home with a stodgy tutor doesn't seem so bad now,' Joachim smiled.

John grimaced. 'Yes, I'd take old Stodgy Face over "Tempesta Horrida" any day.'

'Tempesta Horrida?' Ives looked puzzled. 'Who is that?'

'He's the head of the college – and horrible. We gave him that nickname as it is Latin for frightful storm. Some of the younger boys just have to look at him and they're in floods of tears. He truly is a terrible person. You can understand then why I don't like to have visitors. The college is a cruel, harsh place and on top of that, the sewers pour straight into the streets outside. It smells disgusting. I'm glad to get out when I can and visit my friends.'

John Calvin

'But we hardly ever see you,' Claude complained. 'It must be weeks since you last visited.'

John nodded. Studies were taking up most of his time now.

'So what other strange things go on at that college of yours?' Joachim asked. 'I'm certain that they won't be employing you as an ambassador. You wouldn't do a very good job.'

John laughed, 'Perhaps not. One of the strangest things is that we don't get private confession. We have to publicly confess our sins.'

'What, the whole college together?' Ives exclaimed.

'Yes, you know the ritual, 'I confess to Almighty God, to the blessed Virgin Mary, to blessed Michael the Archangel, to blessed John the Baptist, to the apostles Peter and Paul, to all saints and to you, Father, that I have sinned exceedingly, in thought, word and deed, through my fault, through my own fault, through my most grievous fault… and so on. We all stand there in the hall and say it together. It can get rather noisy!'

At that point, John wondered why the Lord Jesus Christ was not mentioned in the words he'd just said.

'Pierre must have thought it was important enough to mention,' he puzzled. 'Perhaps he thinks that I must confess my sins to Christ?' John shook his head. 'I've heard that a lot of these Reformers have strange new ideas.'

Just then a bell began to toll in the local chapel.

After Darkness Light

'Isn't it about time you left, John?' Claude pointed out.

John nodded, said his goodbyes and wrapping his cowl around his head once more, headed outside to make his way back to the college.

Arriving in time for evening chapel, John stood in the sanctuary listening to the voice of the priest as he prayed to the Virgin Mary. John pondered the fact that it might be he wearing priest's robes and taking confessions in a few years' time. That was the career his father had planned for him.

However, as Calvin mused over his future education, problems were brewing in Noyon and in Europe that would alter Gérard Calvin's plan for his son and change the course of John Calvin's education. With one degree under his belt, John was soon to embark on acquiring another, but not the one that had originally been planned for him.

'Congratulations, John,' Uncle Richard announced. 'I can hardly believe you've graduated. It just seems like yesterday, when you were making your way like a lost puppy along our little street here. You'll soon be going home for a well-earned break, but we hear that you won't be coming back to Paris.'

John shook his uncle's hand and kissed his aunt on the cheek. 'That's right. Father has changed his mind about a career in the church.'

John Calvin

'We were very surprised when we heard that,' Richard exclaimed. 'We thought your father had set his heart on it.'

'And so he had until he fell out with the church leaders at Noyon. I'm not exactly sure what's happened, but there has been a big quarrel. Father has been excommunicated.'

John's aunt gasped at such a drastic action. To be excommunicated was a dreadful punishment. 'If he remains excommunicated they won't allow his body to be buried in holy ground,' she declared.

'Perhaps they'll be able to sort something out,' John's uncle said hopefully.

John sighed, 'I'm not convinced. Any reconciliation may take some time. By all accounts, my father is determined to stand his ground. He insists that the church is being unreasonable and now declares that it is not a good choice of career for me. I'm to change my degree from theology to law and I'll be attending the university at Orléans.'

'Well, John,' admitted his uncle, 'it may be for the best. Your father must be aware of the revolts in Germany and the spread of this Reformation. It may be that the church won't be such a lucrative career for a young man as it once was. You'll certainly find Orléans different from Paris ...'

'Yes, and studying law instead of theology will be quite a change too,' John pointed out. 'I won't grow out my tonsure just yet, though. It is possible to have a career in both law and church which might still happen.'

'You'll be sorry to miss your friends though. I take it the Montmor boys and Claude will be staying on in Paris.'

'Yes. But we're travelling back to Noyon together, which will be fun. I will miss them when I'm in Orléans, but I've a talent for making new friends,' and with that John said goodbye and headed off for a long earned visit home.

As he mounted his horse, to ride over to where he would meet up with the other lads, he could barely keep the excitement off his face. There hadn't been many opportunities to return to Noyon since he had first left. It had been ever so long since John had last seen his family. Extra teaching duties, studies, travelling with the Hangests and then helping other students cram for university entrance exams had all eaten into his vacation time. But at last, he was returning home. He wondered how different the place would be since he had last left.

'Look out for young Pierre when you're there,' John's aunt called after him. 'I hear he's back in Noyon for the summer too.'

John waved and smiled, then went on his way. 'I don't think meeting my young Reformer cousin is such a good idea; not if the current religious climate continues the way it is,' John pondered. 'I hope Pierre realises that it's dangerous to be a Reformer – it could certainly be the ruin of his career, if not the end of his life,' John muttered to himself.

However, all thoughts of careers and Reformation went out of John's head, when he opened a certain door on the Place au Blé and met a much older Antoine, who was nearly a head and shoulders taller than he already. Two young girls in pigtails giggled shyly in a corner. John looked around for his baby sisters and then he realised, 'My, how you've grown,' he gasped.

Mrs Calvin smiled warmly, as the returning student took a look around his old home. 'It's hardly changed a bit,' he exclaimed.

'Well, what were you expecting, son?' Mr Calvin demanded, making his way down the stairs. 'Did you think to find a new wing to the house, with furnishings replaced in every room? I can tell you, we don't have the money for that.'

A bitter edge to his father's voice made John look up anxiously, as he bowed in greeting. Joining him later in the study, he quietly asked after the family finances. 'With the troubles you've been having in the Noyon church, does our family still have enough money to live on? Can you afford to send me to Orléans?'

'Of course I can,' his father grunted. 'We're not in desperation yet. Again, I have to point out to you the value of good connections. If it weren't for our familiarity with the Hangests, we may well have been in poverty. But thankfully, the chaplaincies we received from them, are still in our possession so we remain solvent.'

John breathed a sigh of relief. Even though he had been surprised at his father's change of mind, he was now resigned to it and even looked forward to Orléans.

During the hot summer weeks, John took the opportunity to prepare one or two promising students in Noyon, for entry to the university in the new term and in between teaching assignments, he planned his journey to Orléans. He couldn't, however, avoid meeting up with Pierre, as they had both returned home at the same time ... and on the rare occasions that they bumped into each other, their conversation always seemed to turn round to religion.

John finally got to ask Pierre that question that had been bothering him.

'You say that you don't believe in Purgatory, but surely you must believe in heaven and hell.'

'Of course I do – both places are frequently mentioned in the Bible.'

'There you go, mentioning the Bible again – you'll probably tell me that you actually have a copy – on second thoughts don't tell me anything. I don't want to know. But you admit that you believe in heaven and hell – so tell me, how do you plan to get to heaven? You have no Purgatory to prepare you, to purify you ...'

'No, I have something ... or rather someone far better, the Lord Jesus Christ.'

'What do you mean you have the Lord Jesus Christ? You talk about him as if he were a possession; surely he can't belong to you?'

'Forgive me, cousin, I don't mean to be flippant, but I do believe that I possess the Lord Jesus Christ. I believe he is my Saviour. I believe he is as close to me as my own flesh and soul. I believe what it says in the Scriptures, that he is the only one who can save us from our sins. In Isaiah, it says that our own righteous acts are like filthy rags. When you read those words, it makes the church's teaching seem ridiculous. They say that our good actions, our righteousness, can save us from Purgatory, a place that doesn't exist. But the Bible tells us that our good actions will not save us from hell, a terrible place that certainly does exist. Believe me, John, you must read the Bible for yourself. It is only then that you will see how God's Word tells us of God's gift of salvation.'

John shook his head in bewilderment, as he waved goodbye to his cousin. There weren't many more days before he'd be on his way to Orléans and Pierre would be heading back to Paris. It was a good job, in John's opinion, for his cousin's continual talk about Reform was wearing him down. What strange words he heard from that young man – had he really said that salvation was a gift from God? 'Where does the Bible talk about that?' he wondered.

***

A day or so before his journey to Orléans, Pierre was able to tell him – 'Read Romans chapters six and eight,' he urged.

John considered that request. 'Perhaps I will,' he replied, as Pierre mounted his horse to ride back to Paris. 'Just so that I can prove him wrong,' he muttered, as he returned to his home to organise the final preparations for his travels.

'Life in Orléans will be different from Paris,' a friend wrote to John. 'The student life here is quite free and easy. The sons of the noblemen, flock to the university in order to play tennis, as there are very good courts here. But there are others who take their studies seriously and I'm sure you will be one of them.'

And so he was; any spare time John had in Orléans was spent in study – tennis had no fascination for him whatsoever. Within the year, Calvin became well known by students and faculty alike, as a distinguished scholar. His ability to teach was also recognised and whenever a professor was absent for some reason or other, John Calvin would be called on to teach their classes.

One of the professors became very interested in this aspiring young scholar. Melchior Wolmar had heard that John Calvin planned to join his Greek classes and he was very pleased. A student of that calibre was a welcome addition to any classroom.

John Calvin

Over time the pupil and the professor became firm friends, even though Melchior was a good thirteen years older than John.

One evening, as they sat discussing the previous week's lessons over a glass of wine, Melchior suggested that John might enjoy reading some of Luther's writings.

'Martin Luther, the heretic?' John couldn't believe what he was hearing.

'Yes, *The Liberty of the Christian Man* is an excellent book.' The tutor furtively withdrew one from a desk drawer. 'I'm certain that you will be careful who sees you read it, as they are still burning his works in Paris, I believe.'

John nodded. He had heard of the bonfires that burned books and the other fires that burned people who read the books ... 'But surely these books are of no use to true academics and scholars like us!' he exclaimed.

'Don't dismiss them, John, just because you have heard others despise Luther. Admittedly, the church does not look favourably on him at the moment, but I see in you a sharp enquiring mind. I know that you will read something and come to the truth of it. *The Liberty of the Christian Man* is a worthy title for you to read. It explains Luther's doctrine of justification by faith alone, as well as going into the Marburg Articles.'

John had heard of the Marburg Articles. Very recently Luther and another Reformer, Zwingli, had

had a debate about the Lord's Supper. The Roman Catholics celebrated Mass, while those of a Reformed persuasion had replaced the Mass with what they called the Lord's Supper. Yet, they didn't agree as to whether the real body and blood of Christ were present in the bread and wine. It seemed as though the debate might actually split the new movement in two. There were undoubtedly many in the Roman Catholic Church who were eagerly anticipating it.

'I'll read it,' John agreed, 'because you ask me to. However, you may as well know that I am not a Reformer nor likely to be.'

Melchior smiled, 'I couldn't make you one even if I wanted to. However, you may as well know that I am a Reformer, but as well as that, I hope to be your friend.'

Calvin smiled. What was it about those Reformation men? First it was Pierre, now Melchior.

And then there was Light

When a weary and travel-soiled Pierre arrived on Calvin's doorstep, in Orléans, he was very surprised to see his Roman Catholic cousin reading a Martin Luther book.

'What are you doing here, Pierre?' his cousin gasped, as he ushered the exhausted young man into his lodgings.

'Haven't you heard?' Pierre coughed as he tried to warm himself at the fire. 'Persecutions have begun in Paris once more – it's not safe to be a Reformer in our capital city. I was told to run for my life. I hope to begin my studies again in Orléans. This is a much safer city than Paris.'

John sighed as he hung his cousin's cape by the fire, to get the chill out of it. 'How many times have I warned you to be careful, Pierre …?'

But just then Pierre glanced over at Calvin's desk, where a pile of books was stacked up against the wall. One particular volume was sitting on the top.

'If I'm not mistaken, John, you are reading *The Liberty of the Christian Man*?'

'Yes,' Calvin nodded. 'I should not have left it sitting there. Here I am giving warnings to you, yet I

67

leave heretical books lying around for anybody to see. But, cousin, I'd like to know what you think of this justification by faith alone.'

'You know me well enough, John. I am for it!' Pierre smiled.

Their conversation went on long into the night, and continued during the other nights after that. Conversations with Melchior also helped to clear John's thinking about the issue. At last, he realised how crucial this doctrine was to the Reformed faith. It was central to it, a key difference between it and the Roman Catholic Church.

'Let's go over this once again,' he asked his cousin, Pierre, one afternoon. 'Explain this justification to me again.'

'Very well ... I suppose the best place to begin is the beginning,' Pierre suggested. 'So let's go back to Genesis. You have heard about Adam and Eve. They were the first humans, created by God, and lived in a perfect world, unstained by any sin. But they disobeyed God and that was when our troubles began.'

John nodded. He had heard this story at his mother's knee, how Adam and Eve had eaten the forbidden fruit and had been banished from the beautiful garden for ever.

Pierre carried on, 'That is why we are sinners today. God's perfect standard was broken and humanity's basic nature became sinful. The Bible says that we are sinners from the moment we begin to exist in our mother's womb. Sin is woven into the very fabric of our being. To be a human being means that you are a sinner. Romans 3:23 tells us that all have sinned and fallen short of the glory of God. No one living is righteous before God. You can read that in Psalm 143.'

'Yes, I have heard that Psalm before. It was one of the ones they read to us in the college at dinner time, but I don't believe they ever read from the book of Romans, at least not that I remember.'

'Well, I can't spend all my time going through the whole of Scripture, but if you were to read it for yourself,' he added pointedly, 'you would read of the people of Israel, throughout the Old Testament, who made sacrifices to God to atone for their sins. These were sacrifices of pure and spotless lambs. However, every year a new lamb was required. The sacrifices that were made were not enough to deal with sin once and for all – they had to be repeated. God had instructed his people to sacrifice these lambs, so that one day they would recognise the true Lamb of God, who would come to save his people from their sins. These lambs, in the Old Testament times, were like signposts pointing to the one true sacrifice which would come. That one true sacrifice would be the Lord Jesus Christ – God's own Son.'

John was leaning forward in his chair. His cousin's speech was interesting. He was keen to hear more.

'Well, the years went by, and the prophets came and went. One of these prophets, or messengers from God, was Isaiah who said, "He is despised and rejected of men; a man of sorrows and acquainted with grief, and we hid as it were our faces from him, he was despised and we esteemed him not. Surely he has borne our griefs and carried our sorrows: yet we did esteem him stricken, smitten of God and afflicted. But he was wounded for our transgressions, he was bruised for our iniquities, the chastisement of our peace was upon him, and with his stripes we are healed."

'David also spoke in Psalm 22 of one who would be mocked and pierced.

'The prophet Micah spoke of how a great ruler would be born in the insignificant village of Bethlehem.

'You might not know it, but these words written hundreds of years before Jesus Christ was born, are actually prophecies about him, prophecies that would come true when he lived and died among us.

'You can read in the New Testament about how the Saviour of the world was born to a virgin in the town of Bethlehem. Years later, at the River Jordan, John the Baptist announces, "Behold the Lamb of God, who takes away the sin of the world."'

'Ah yes,' John exclaimed. 'I see how that links back to the Old Testament sacrifices. I see that … the one true sacrifice … hmm … interesting.'

Pierre continued. 'Then again in the New Testament we come to Calvary; we see the Son of God despised and rejected by mankind; even his closest friends desert him. We see him there smitten, bruised and scourged ... and our minds can go back to the prophet Isaiah and we realise that here we have the fulfilment of those words that were spoken by God centuries before.

'Soldiers mock him and nail him to a cross and our minds go back to Psalm 22. It all fits. It all ties in together. What do you think it means, John, when the Bible says that he was wounded for our transgressions, bruised for our iniquities and that with his stripes we are healed? Who is Isaiah talking about?'

John thought silently, not answering. 'It must mean Jesus Christ,' he thought to himself.

'Surely it means,' Pierre continued, 'that Christ's death and suffering has healed his people from their sins. It is Jesus that Isaiah was talking about. If the Word of God is telling us that Jesus Christ's death has successfully dealt with the sin of his people, then surely there is no need for penance and Purgatory.

'We can trust in God's Son to free us from sin and give us eternal life. The prophecies focus on Jesus Christ. The Gospel stories tell us that it was JESUS who died to save his people.

'It wasn't Mary on the cross. It wasn't one of the numberless Roman Catholic saints who suffered to bring salvation.

'Jesus Christ was the only one capable of bringing salvation, as he is the only sinless Son of God! Saints and sanctuaries have nothing to do with it!'

These new thoughts were strange, terrifying and somehow wonderful to John, as well. A shiver went down his spine, whether through fear or thrill he didn't know.

Pierre was in full flow, however. John concentrated hard on what his cousin had to say. 'Now, Luther talks about justification and as you're studying law, John, I'm sure you have a better understanding of that legal term than I do. What does it mean to you?'

John drummed his fingers on the table as he gathered his thoughts together. 'If you are justified it means that you have been declared righteous and are not liable to any penalty. I suppose you could say that the person who is justified is entitled to all the privileges given to a person who has kept the law. The judge is pronouncing a sentence that is opposite to what the criminal deserves. I can't say that I've often come across this sort of situation in any of my legal papers.'

Pierre nodded, 'I'm sure you haven't; it would be a famous case if indeed it did exist. But do you remember when I told you to read Romans chapter 6? Let me repeat some of it to you now, "For the wages of sin is death, but the gift of God is eternal life through Jesus Christ our Lord."'

'I'm interested in that word gift, Pierre,' John interrupted.

'I thought you would be; it is an important word, simply because gifts are free. No father gives his child a present and expects him to pay for it. God is the same; he doesn't expect money from you or anyone else in exchange for the gift of eternal life. He offers you a gift; all he expects of you is to take it with thanks.

'But let's get back to that word justify. Further on it says in Romans 8:33, "Who shall bring any charge against God's elect? It is God who justifies. Who is to condemn? Christ Jesus is the one who died, more than that, who was raised, who is at the right hand of God, who indeed is interceding for us." You should really read the rest of that chapter, John, it is truly wonderful.

'But look at these words. Jesus is interceding for us, not Mary, not the saints! It's there in black and white in God's Word.

'And it's God who justifies us. We cannot save ourselves.

'Now it's important that you realise that justification is not the change that happens gradually to those who trust in God. When God renews us and gives us new desires, that is what we call sanctification, not justification. When God justifies us, he deals with our sin once and for all. This is what happened at the cross. Justification is a gift from God. When God justifies his people, he is giving them a new status.'

'A new status?' John asked, puzzled.

'Yes. In Romans 8:14 it says that all who are led by the Spirit of God are sons of God. When God justifies his people, he is adopting them into his own family.

That is their new status. All the sins of our past are done away with and our future in eternity is secure, because with his stripes we are healed, remember! So, yet more words of Scripture that prove that Purgatory does not exist.'

John looked at his cousin thoughtfully, 'One day I was going to ask you a question, only I never got round to doing it. I was going to ask you how you thought we could get into heaven without Purgatory. We can't get into heaven for free, surely? Someone has to suffer.'

'But, John!' Pierre exclaimed. 'That's what I've been trying to say. We can get into heaven for free, because Jesus has paid the price for us at the cross. When he was crucified and left killed by the Romans, he was also fulfilling God the Father's plan. He was dying and suffering in our place.

'Yes, someone has to suffer, but it's not us. Jesus has done all the suffering for us. We cannot purchase our place in heaven through penance and pilgrimage. The purchasing of eternal life has been done by Christ, at the cross. All that we need to do is to ask God to forgive our sins through his Son, Jesus Christ, for it is God who loves us and has given his Son for our salvation.

'The Gospel of John says in chapter 3, "God so loved the world, that he gave his one and only Son, that whosoever believes in him should not perish, but have everlasting life."'

Pierre poured another glass of ale before continuing, 'We are sinners, you and I, and as sinners the law of God makes certain demands on us. God's law must be obeyed and a penalty must be paid for those sins that we commit. Now you know how hard it is not to sin.'

John nodded. 'Even as a child I would wonder at the many sins I committed. Each time I went to confession I would have a brand-new list of misdemeanours. It was as if I couldn't stop myself.'

Pierre sighed and scratched his head. 'That is so true, John. As I said, sin is in the very fabric of our being. We battle with it, but even then we lose, especially if we are fighting it on our own, without God's help. When we think about the sins we have already committed there is no way we could endure the penalty that those sins deserve.'

'How then can we be given access to heaven?' John exclaimed.

'Listen to me, John. I'll say it once again. What you have to do is to trust in Christ and his sacrifice. Jesus lived a perfect life on earth, and he did this because we fail at it. He paid the penalty that we should have paid, when he died upon the cross. He did this, because someone had to take the punishment for sin, and as sinners we are woefully inadequate for the job.

'In Galatians 3:13, it says that Christ redeemed us from the curse of the law by becoming a curse for us.'

'What a thought!' Calvin whispered, almost inaudibly.

'Indeed,' his cousin replied, 'but I would say, "What a truth!"'

The candle in the corner flickered as a breeze found its way under the door. John moved it to a more sheltered spot before sitting down again.

'So what you are saying is that God the Father is giving us eternal life, because his Son has taken the punishment that was meant for us, when he died on the cross. Why would God do that?'

'Oh, I can hardly begin to understand the gracious character of God ...' Pierre exclaimed, 'but here is an amazing truth; salvation for God's people was planned from the very beginning.

'The Bible says that, even before the earth was formed, God had designed this wonderful work of salvation. God knew that humanity would sin against him, yet he had such mercy that he planned to deliver them, even before he had created them.

'He gave his Son to be our Saviour, even before he had created the world that we would spoil through our selfishness and greed.

'God the Father gave God the Son as a Saviour for his people because he loves his people, but also because it glorifies God; it shows the world and all of creation that he is righteous and merciful.'

'It just seems so incredible,' John spoke out. 'What you are saying is that when you trust in Christ to forgive you for your sins, there isn't anything left for you to do.'

Pierre's eyes lit up. 'Yes, that is exactly what I am saying. Our sin is put on Christ and his righteousness is put on us. Do you remember the words that Christ said on the cross – the very last words?'

'He said, "It is finished,"' John replied.

'You have to believe then that Christ's work really is finished. He went through the pain, the suffering, the separation from God and completed what needed to be done. He didn't leave things unfinished – it is finished. The work of salvation was completed at the cross. Jesus has done it all. You don't have to do anything, just trust God.'

'Trust God,' Calvin mused. 'That's what that phrase means, by faith alone.'

'Yes, remember though it's not your faith that justifies you, it's not your faith that makes you righteous in God's eyes. It is God that makes you righteous, when you have faith in his Son, Jesus Christ.

'John,' Pierre asked earnestly, 'do you trust in Jesus or are you still trying to work your way back to God? If you are still trying to justify yourself, rest assured it won't happen. There is nothing you can do in your own strength that will make you right with God. You must have your sin dealt with. God is the only one who can do this.

'To get right with God, it's not about what you can do for yourself, but it is about trusting in what

God has already done for you, through his Son at Calvary. You come to God the Father to ask him for forgiveness, because you trust in what Jesus Christ, his Son, has done on the cross.'

John quietly nodded his head. Pierre, wise to his cousin's need to be left alone to think, and hopefully to pray, patted him on the back and took his leave.

That evening, as John rearranged his books, he carefully put Luther's title at the back of the pile along with one or two others that might be looked on by the authorities as undesirable. 'Erasmus,' John muttered as he picked up that famous author's work, 'He taught at Montaigu at one point. There is a passage in this book where he is quite sharp about penance. Yes, here it is, "Perhaps you believe that all your sins are washed away with a little piece of paper, a sealed parchment, the gift of a little money, some wax image or a little pilgrimage. You are utterly deceived ..."'

John's heart lurched ... he remembered the relief he had felt about his mother's pilgrimage to the abbey at Ourscamp. Now he realised, that so many of the foundations that he'd trusted in were false hopes. He could see that now, but did that mean that the church that he had grown up in was completely false? John wasn't sure.

'I've been taught all my life that, to obtain salvation, I had to pay God back for my sins. I had to work in order to be allowed into heaven. But I should have realised all the work I did made no difference;

I kept sinning and so I had to keep working. It was never ending. In the past, whenever I have thought about my sins, or thought about my God, I have been reduced to a quivering wreck, completely terrified. It has only been through these new books and Pierre and Melchior's discussions, that I have begun to see a new way ... a true way.'

John shook his head in bewilderment. Here he was, admitting that his Reformed friends might actually be right. 'They may have been telling me the truth all this time ... and all this time I have been listening to the truth, curious, intrigued, but refusing to believe. But how can I abandon the church, the church I have grown up with, that I respect?'

Calvin stood and looked out of his window at the stars, a thin sliver of a moon shone in the midnight sky. 'But if I am truthful, this church that I respect, does not deserve my respect,' John sighed. 'I can see now that I have been taught lies. I have been living a life that is simply wrong, doing wrong things, thinking wrong things, believing wrong things. Somehow tonight, I can see all this, whereas before I didn't. Has someone turned a light on inside my head? So often, I refused to read God's Word, I wonder what God must think of me for being so dismissive of his truth?'

At that thought, a shiver went down John's spine, a shiver of fear. He knew that he had to do something, he had to seek forgiveness for his sins from the only one who could forgive him, the one he had sinned against.

After Darkness Light

John kneeled and prayed, 'Oh Lord, I am a wretch and I earnestly ask you that you do not judge me as I deserve. I have in the past abandoned your Word, but I know now that this is a wonderful gift to me. I ask you, Lord, to forgive my sins. I have been in terrible darkness, but my Lord and Saviour, I ask you now to send me light.'

And after the darkness there was light; it was gradual in many ways. Over time, in Orléans and later as he studied in Bourges, Calvin learned more of God's Word and more of the Reformed faith. He preached occasionally in villages around Orléans, because his faith in Christ and his study of God's Word were not things that he could keep to himself.

John realised more and more, that this was a new life he was leading, with new passions and new faith. Now that he knew that the Bible was a book to be read, John felt as though he had tasted something new and refreshing. He felt compelled to read more and more and more.

'There is no better guide for my life,' he declared one morning as he opened the Bible once again. 'No church, no parent, no scholar even could ever guide my life in the way God's Word does.'

Reformer on the Run

One morning, as Calvin hastily packed some belongings and tied them to the back of his horse, he cast his mind back over the years. 'I owe my father so much,' he sighed, 'it is hard to picture a world without him.'

The year was 1531 and Calvin was now in his early twenties. He had just heard news that the man who had attempted to guide most of his life up to that point, had suddenly fallen desperately ill. Gérard Calvin was in danger of losing his life. John was summoned home urgently. Many doctors were called for and consulted, but the illness progressed steadily. Eventually, John and his family realised that there was nothing that could be done. Twelve days after John arrived back at Noyon, his father passed away.

The funeral took place eventually, but not until after Charles and John had pleaded with the church authorities for their father to be buried in holy ground.

John wondered if he should spend so much time dealing with these superstitions; but the issue of holy ground meant a lot to the other members of his family. It meant that his father would be buried within the church cemetery. Burial outside the cemetery was a public disgrace and something to be ashamed of. Many believed that, if you were buried outside holy ground, you would never be allowed into heaven.

John now knew, however, that these superstitions were not true. He would miss his father, but there was nothing he could do for him now. His eternal future had always been in the hands of God.

Some time after the burial, John began to realise something. 'I can study what I choose. I could give up the law.'

'Why would you give up the law?' Charles demanded.

'I hate all the arguments and conflicts. You know the sort of thing, fighting this case and that case. It's not what I want at all.'

'Are you just going to leave without your degree? That really would be a waste.'

'No, I've got the degree, not long before I left for Noyon, in fact. But I don't have to be a lawyer. I'm thinking of going back to Paris. I'd like to study the classics.'

Charles patted John on the back and smiled. 'Yes, you are definitely the clever one in the family. And if you're going to head back to Paris, you can travel with Antoine. He's living there now.'

John smiled. It would be good to get to know Antoine again and he looked forward to being able to study what he wanted to for a change.

***

Paris was the same as ever, but different too. It was busy and bustling, people thronging the streets and pushing their wares in the markets. New buildings seemed to spring up where old ones had been knocked down. His old college, Montaigu, was still there as it had been for many, many years before Calvin had ever set eyes on it. And it was across the road from his old college, that he found his new lodgings. 'I'll put up with the awful smells,' he told Antoine. 'It means that the rent is cheaper.'

Antoine nodded, 'Yes ... I hear that Charles hasn't been that efficient about arranging the family finances.'

John sighed, 'I'll have to be frugal, I know, but I've been used to that before. My days as a student at Montaigu were a good training ground for that. As well as that, my first book will be printed this year.'

'Well, that's good,' his younger brother tried to sound encouraging. 'You might make some money from that.'

'Said like someone who has no knowledge of publishing,' John grimaced. 'I have to pay for the publication of this book out of my own pocket.'

It was just the beginning of Calvin's involvement with the printing press, but it was not a book that was that well received. Other writings that he would construct in the future, would receive more praise and more criticism.

After Darkness Light

Paris wasn't his permanent abode during that time either. He went back to Orléans for some time in 1532 and took with him a copy of the Bible in French! A brief visit to Noyon and then he was back to Paris once again. The freedom to make his own decisions, was something he was taking firm advantage of. But Calvin was becoming more and more concerned about the lack of freedoms given to those who were of the Reformed persuasion.

Religious conflicts increased in Paris. The king's sister was a supporter of the Protestant cause and often pleaded with her brother to save Reformed believers, who were sentenced to death for their 'crimes'. Those who supported Roman Catholicism were furious at her. Paris was heating up.

And it was at that point, that a close friend of Calvin's was called upon to make a speech. Nicolas Cop was the rector of the university, a dedicated Reformer and a supporter of Luther. Calvin was asked to give his friend some advice about what he should say at this highly charged time in the capital's history.

'You'll end up writing this speech,' Nicolas grinned, as they sat down yet again to discuss what should be said. Calvin laughed, but that is indeed what happened. In this speech he admonished the listeners, who were learned theologians, about how their discussions mentioned nothing about faith or the love of God. They neither discussed the forgiveness of sins, grace or justification. He accused them of drowning

John Calvin

these real doctrines under their own petty laws. 'I beg of you all, here present, never to sit back and accept these heresies, these insults against God.'

Calvin may have written the speech, but it was Nicolas Cop who delivered it and it was he who had to flee afterwards. The speech was publicly burned, but Nicolas Cop wasn't and escaped with his life.

However, it wasn't long before Calvin too fell under suspicion.

'He was one of the rector's closest friends and was often to be seen discussing things with him privately. Very suspicious ...'

'He's one of those Reformers for certain. He never says anything against Luther these days.'

'I'm sure he's reading the Bible ... we just can't prove it.'

Then one day, an anxious colleague burst into John's narrow room, his face flushed, gasping for breath. John frantically looked up from his books and papers. 'Flee for your life, John,' was the urgent request as the noise began to escalate in the corridor outside. 'The others will keep the guards at the door for as long as they can, but you have to get out now!'

John looked right and left — what could he take with him, his books, his papers?

'Just go! We'll get your books and papers to you somehow, but right now your life is in danger.'

Between them, the two young men made a sturdy rope out of a pair of curtains, in order to lower

John out the window where he could run to safety at a friend's house. There he was disguised as a vine dresser and began a life of wandering from town to town, in his attempts to escape capture.

He never did see his books and papers again, but at least he was free.

Calvin flitted here and there, sometimes at Noyon, then at Orléans, then again in Poitiers. He was sheltered by friends and family and by anyone who sympathised with the Reformed faith. In the midst of all his troubles, John still found the time to write, this time explaining the error behind what the Anabaptists thought happened to Christians when they died. 'They do not fall asleep until the resurrection,' was Calvin's decree. 'The souls of those who die in the faith of Christ, live in Christ.'

Calvin was definitely a Reformer now. In 1534, he travelled to Angoulême and began writing, what would be one of his life's major works called, *The Institutes of the Christian Religion*. John could see how hungry people were to hear the truth about God and not just popish superstitions.

'What I am writing might very well mean I shall lose my life, but the people need to hear the truth. And books are such a great way to get the truth out into the world. And what a truth it is!

'*It is my firm belief that we should not seek out God anywhere else than in his sacred Word or to think anything about him that is not prompted by his Word or speak anything that is not taken from that Word. It is an audacity to rashly turn Scripture in any way we please. The Bible is not a sport; it is of all things the most sacred on earth.'*

In that same year, John also journeyed to Nérac where he met with a man named Jacques Lefèvre, the one who had translated the New Testament into French. It was quite a year of change for John. He had become certain in the Reformed faith and during a trip to Noyon, gave up all the chaplaincies that were his only source of income. Now he was totally dependent on what his friends and family could supply him with, or what he could earn from writing or teaching.

Even though it was a dangerous place, he managed a brief stay in Paris before returning to Angoulême. John had decided to visit the city for one reason, to meet a man named Michael Servetus, who had published a book that spoke out against the Trinity.

In a world where many innocent people were being accused of being heretics, here was a man who definitely was one. Calvin agreed to debate with Michael and journeyed to Paris, even though he risked his life in doing so.

He needn't have bothered, as Servetus didn't even keep their appointment. Calvin's hopes to change Servetus' mind were overturned.

During his stay in Paris, it was a dear friend of his, Etienne de la Forge, who looked after him. He was just another example of the many committed Reformers, who were willing to risk their lives to help those who preached the true Word of God.

But as Calvin left Paris once more, the city was on the verge of meltdown. All it took was one French pastor and a large printing of pamphlets and the whole country, not just the capital, was in an uproar.

What the pamphlets said was quite right. They spoke out against the Mass and other heresies of the Roman Church, but, perhaps unwisely, the pastor wrote words that were antagonistic in their tone.

He posted these pamphlets everywhere and even put one on the bedroom door of the king himself. A wiser man might not have been so disrespectful to his monarch. The king was now furious – not even his Protestant sister could soothe his temper.

The news of the national uproar soon arrived in Angoulême and at John Calvin's lodgings. His landlord, out of breath and almost choking in his urgency to speak, sat down exhausted on a chair in the kitchen. Calvin, who had just been getting ready to go out, could see that there was something far wrong. Something dreadful must have happened.

'It's Paris. There have been burnings in Paris,' Louis gasped.

John judged by the grey pallor of his friend's face, that the burnings were not of books and speeches.

'What is it, Louis?' John asked. 'What has happened? Tell me everything.'

John Calvin

Louis du Tillet slumped in his chair and soon John was familiar with the fresh news from the capital city.

'Twenty executions?' Calvin gasped.

'That is what I've been told. Over the last three months, they've been arresting people left, right and centre, but I never thought there would be as many deaths as this. There is worse news than that, though, John.'

Louis looked at his friend; a deep frown across his forehead told John that his friend did not want to be the one to share this next report with him.

'Your friend, Etienne de la Forge, was one of the twenty.'

At this, John also sat down; the news was indeed hard to hear.

'That man was as kind a friend as I ever had in Paris. I lodged with him briefly and he was generous enough to take a penniless Christian into his home for safekeeping. Oh Louis – all this persecution and now the burnings ... For a while I felt that the Roman Catholic Church might be reformed from inside, but now it is clear that it is rotten. I believe it must be a lost cause for us ...'

Louis shook his head in sympathy. 'They say that there is no safe place for a Lutheran in Paris now ... perhaps not even in France. There is even a royal edict out against us. John, both you and I need to make plans to save our own lives. Can we leave the country, do you think?'

'Yes,' John agreed, 'we should leave and quickly. How soon can you be ready?'

'I can be ready by the end of today. How about you?'

'The same. I suggest that we leave immediately for Basel. Not long ago, I heard that my cousin, Pierre, has escaped there from the persecutions in Orléans. There are other Reformers there also – William Farel is one of them. Erasmus is now a resident of that town. There are already several intellectuals who have chosen Basel as a refuge. It is one of those few cities that we can call Reformed.'

Louis was already getting up out of his chair, picking up books and papers, calling for his servant to pack clothes, food and other supplies.

'We leave France tonight, then,' Louis declared.

John nodded. 'There is a need more than ever for my book,' he said to himself, as he thought about the notes and papers he would have to pack with care. 'I believe Basel will be as good a place as any to publish it,' he sighed. 'Though I hadn't planned to publish it so soon, it needs to be done. The Lord's people require it.'

Basel and Books

'Cousin,' came the cry from across the street. Calvin looked up. He had been expecting to see Pierre in Basel, but he hadn't expected him to come out to meet him, on his arrival in the city.

'Pierre! How good it is to see you at last!'

'I take it your journey wasn't too arduous?' Pierre enquired.

At this, John sighed. 'No, leaving my native land was remarkably easy, despite the fact that my servant ran off with all my funds. Thankfully, Louis had enough money to take us the rest of the journey to Basel, but here I am homeless and penniless once again.'

'Well, don't worry,' Pierre smiled. 'There may be something I can do about the pennies at least.'

'And what might that be?' John asked.

'Come and work for me.'

And that is exactly what John did. Pierre was translating an edition of the entire Bible – not just the New Testament. As a Hebrew scholar he would translate the Old Testament, but he also wanted to edit Lefranc's edition of the New Testament. 'You'd be ideal for that, John. You've got excellent Latin and Greek.'

John nodded. 'I'd be glad to do that, but have you heard that I'm also writing something of my own?'

'I had heard a rumour, cousin. What exactly is it?'

'I'm calling it *The Institutes of the Christian Religion*. I am writing down, for the first time, the essential truths of the Reformed faith for people to read.'

Pierre grinned from ear to ear. 'I am definitely looking forward to discussing that with you. We are going to have some good evenings round my fireplace, I can tell you. I always enjoyed our conversations, dear cousin, but I have a feeling that our best ones are yet to come. Have you heard though that the Protestant Princes of Germany have openly criticised King Francis for his treatment of the Reformers?'

John shook his head. 'I hadn't heard that, but I am glad to. Friends of mine have perished in the recent persecutions. I'm afraid Paris is not what it used to be, or France either.'

Pierre lifted up his cousin's bags and led him towards some livery stables. 'Well, we will have to wait and see what King Francis says in reply. I am certain that he will, for no king can stomach a criticism without sniping back in some way.'

And that was exactly what happened. A disgruntled French king stomped his feet and wrote back to the Protestant princes, that he was totally just in treating his Protestant citizens in this way. They were an unruly bunch of Reformers out to destroy his kingdom. In Francis' opinion the German princes didn't understand the troubles he had to bear. The German Protestants were obviously a much more placid people and not such a trouble to their royalty.

Calvin could not hear of his sovereign's response and remain silent.

'I am going to insert a preface to *The Institutes* – a direct plea to King Francis.'

'Is that wise?' Pierre asked John. 'Might it not cause more trouble?'

But John was already showing that he had a wise head for leadership and an astute understanding of how best to put forward his ideas. The preface to this first major work, was an example of how to alert someone to his errors in a respectful way. Calvin used his ability as a theologian and as a lawyer to good effect.

He demanded justice for the Reformers, explaining how they were the true church, as the Roman Catholic Church had deserted the teachings of the New Testament.

Calvin pointed out that, though the Roman Catholic Church accused the Reformers of having a faith that was new, unknown and uncertain, this was totally untrue. The faith of the Reformers was not new, it was straight out of Scripture. It was not unknown as it was straight from the New Testament. It was not uncertain, as Calvin was so sure of its truth that he did not fear death or even God's judgement seat.

On reading the first draft of the preface, Pierre sat down and slowly began to nod his head in agreement.

'Whether he will read it or not I can't say, but you should put it in whatever.'

'I plan to include another paragraph. The Roman Catholic Church says that our faith lacks authentic miracles. What they fail to realise is that there are authentic miracles in the Bible. We do not need others. It is only Rome, who has abandoned the teachings of the New Testament, that needs further miracles.'

'Warn the king also, not to believe all these false charges against Reformers,' Pierre pleaded.

'Yes,' John acknowledged. 'I will do that. They are accused of being rebels when they actually lead quiet, simple lives, often praying for their king.'

'Absolutely,' Pierre declared. 'If this is just the preface, then I can't wait to read the rest of the work. You must finish it as soon as possible.'

'I believe my final draft is complete.'

An eager Pierre looked at his cousin and smiled. 'May I?' he asked tentatively.

'May you be the first to read it?'

'Please,' he begged and Calvin relented.

Pierre buried his nose in the pile of papers that John gave him and did not come out again until long after Calvin had been sound asleep in his bed.

The following morning, John asked his cousin what he thought.

'Excellent,' was his reply.

'Can you summarise it for me?' John asked. 'I want to know if I have put my points across clearly.'

John Calvin

'Well, you have written about six different points as far as I can see,' Pierre wrinkled up his forehead as he organised his thoughts. 'I suppose one section is on the law of God. That is where you explain about sin and how the human race has become totally corrupt.'

'Yes,' John reached over to point out a sentence or two, 'you will have noticed I talk about how any human effort to gain righteousness, is useless.'

Pierre nodded. 'You then go on to describe how God's law is like a looking glass. When we read it, God shows us what we are like – that we are sinners. After you discuss the Ten Commandments, you sum up that section by arguing that God's law has three main uses – to restrain sinful mankind in their daily lives, to convict sinners and show them their need of Christ and then to provide a guide for how to live.'

'Well, you've got the first point at any rate,' Calvin agreed, as he sat down beside his cousin at the kitchen table. 'What's next?'

'Faith. You show that there is a difference between knowing in your head that God exists and believing in him.'

'Go on,' Calvin urged. 'Explain that a bit further.'

'You talk about how you can read the Bible and believe that these things happened, that there was a flood, that David killed Goliath, that Jesus and the disciples performed miracles, but that this is not the belief that saves. The belief that saves, is when you put all your hope and confidence in God and in Christ.

After Darkness Light

It's just like what we've discussed on many other occasions – the only truth we can rely on is the truth that God has given us in his Word. You then explain the Trinity.'

Calvin poured a drink of milk from a jug on the table. 'Yes, that's why I'll be sending Servetus a copy. He needs clear teaching on the Trinity before he causes some real trouble with his heresies. That's why I believe books like this are important. Truthful teachings about Christian doctrines are essential to stop people from swallowing lies.'

Pierre turned over one of the pages on the table before him. 'Ah yes, you cover prayer next, how we are to pray to God alone in the name of Christ. We don't need to go through the saints and indeed we shouldn't, for that in itself is wrong. After that, you explain Baptism and the Lord's Supper.'

'That's right. We call them sacraments, an external sign that God uses to show goodwill to his people in order to strengthen their weak faith,' Calvin explained. 'The Roman Catholic Church teaches that there are several sacraments, but in fact there are only two: Baptism and the Lord's Supper.'

'It is good,' Pierre pointed out, 'that you go on to explain what the Lord's Supper is. I noticed that you have a different point of view from Luther and Zwingli.'

'That's right. Zwingli believes that it's simply a ceremony to remind us that the Lord died for us. But I cannot agree with that. There is certainly something

John Calvin

spiritual about remembering the Lord's death with the bread and wine. But since Christ's body is in heaven and a physical body can only be in one place, his body and blood cannot be physically present in the communion bread and wine. However, Christ is still present at the Supper in a true way – in a helpful way. That is why I believe we should celebrate the Lord's Supper once every week, at least!' Calvin added.

'You then go on to criticise some of the practices of the Roman Catholic Church, such as indulgences, Purgatory, the holy orders.'

John interrupted at that point. 'Holy orders are offices that have been devised by the Roman Church, but the Bible only recognises one – simply someone who is a preacher of the Word of God.'

'How am I doing so far then, John?' Pierre asked cheerfully.

'Well enough, cousin,' John joked. 'But I believe you have one more point to cover.'

'How could I forget?' Pierre smiled. 'Christian liberty. You teach about how Christians submit to God's law, not because they are forced to, but because they obey the law of God voluntarily. They want to thank God, so that is why they obey him. They love him, so they demonstrate their love for him by being obedient to him. God's law is the rule for our life, but he gives us a liberty to make our own minds up about things, that are not specifically against God's law such as laughing, food, music, wine …'

'That's right,' John consented. 'Humanity has two governments in the world ... a spiritual government and an earthly government. Christ is the only King of the spiritual government and the Scriptures the only law. Even if a church council goes against God's Word, we should not obey it. We should only obey those councils when they are in agreement with the Word of God.'

'Then you go on to talk about the earthly government and that it has been established by God for the peace of the people. Even if we have a ruler who is vicious and a tyrant, we must obey his laws unless his laws go against God's law. If they do then we must respectfully disobey him.'

'A good summary of my work Pierre, it proves at least that you have read most of it and understood some of it.'

Pierre laughed. 'Get the book published as soon as you can, John. You can then send it to King Francis and Michael Servetus, but there are many more people than that who need to read it.'

Calvin sighed. Now there was a truth! But how would he get these books, once published, into the hands of those who longed to read their words? Bonfires were being lit in every Roman Catholic town to burn Reformed books like his and to kill those who read them.

Geneva – Part One

Some time later, those worries and concerns sent Calvin on yet another journey, to Italy. Louis went with him as they visited the Duchess Renée, in order to plead with her to help them in their fight for the rights of the Reformers.

Weeks later, as John and Louis left Italy, it was in an even more sombre mood. Their journey had been fruitless; the duchess was unable to help them.

When John and Louis arrived in Basel once more, John looked on in sorrow as his friend turned his horse around and headed for the city gates. Louis was leaving, and returning to Angoulême with plans to head for Geneva in the near future. Calvin suspected that it was not just a city he was leaving, but a faith. However, with *The Institutes* finally published, Calvin decided that it would be best if he went back to his studies, this time in Strasbourg. He set off for Noyon to sort out some family business and then he picked up Antoine and Marie, his half-sister, in Paris. All three Calvin siblings were going to set up home together once again. Charles did not come with them.

Riding along a hot and dusty road with all their belongings, John Calvin was pleased to be part of a family once again. But he was concerned about Charles, whom they were leaving behind. 'He is furious with the Roman Catholic Church at the moment, but he doesn't commit himself to the Reformation either. Maybe he will in the future. We'll have to wait and see.'

John turned to smile at his young sister, who was already finding the travelling difficult. 'I'm sorry that the journey is going to be much longer than usual. The war between Francis and King Charles of Spain means that we have to make a long detour south.'

Marie sighed. Travel at any time was tiring and uncomfortable, but in the middle of July, weeks on the road, on horseback, would certainly not be pleasant.

'There is one small consolation,' John told her. 'I hope we may get the opportunity to pay a short visit to the city of Geneva, on our journey to Strasbourg.'

However, the stay in Geneva would be for a lot longer than Calvin had planned and would have an abrupt end. Strange things like this quite often happened to Reformers in those days.

Martin Bucer stood at the entrance to his house in Strasbourg, in order to give a warm welcome to the city's newest pastor. The year was 1538, so it had taken Calvin a lot longer than a month to reach Strasbourg; it had taken him almost two years. When Calvin finally met with Martin Bucer, he felt as though he was meeting both a friend and a stranger. He was familiar with Martin's writings and had learned much from him, but this was a man he had never met before.

However, Martin Bucer had heard much about John Calvin and realised that, with the right guidance, this brilliant young scholar would be just the right person to start up the first French-speaking Protestant congregation in Strasbourg.

'You've finally arrived,' he declared, as a weary Calvin dismounted his horse and reached over to shake his hand.

And with that comment, Calvin's mind flitted back over the last two years, scene by scene. He had arrived in Geneva two years ago with plans to leave it, but he had soon been forced to stay. Then, just a few weeks ago he had been forced to leave the city just when he had had plans to prosper it. A lot had happened in between his arrival in Geneva and his exit.

He had arrived in Geneva with a simple plan for an overnight stay, nothing more. 'I may have time to visit my friend, Louis, who has moved recently to the city, but other than that, I have not many acquaintances in Geneva.'

However, John's brief visit to his old friend meant that, before he could stop it, the news that John Calvin was in the city had spread far and wide. It soon reached the ears of the Reformer, William Farel.

He had once been in Basel, but now was one of the many Reformers who had made their way to

After Darkness Light

Geneva. This old preacher had a reputation for being a strong and demanding character. Some described him as 'bombastic', others as 'fearless'. He was, without doubt, a courageous Reformation preacher, though perhaps a bit disorganised. Several years before Calvin's arrival in the city, Farel had turned up to begin the work of bringing the city to the truth of God's Word. Now he felt that he was in need of an assistant and that young John Calvin was just the ticket.

Calvin's meeting with Farel, on his overnight stop, was to be one of those moments that changed the direction of John's life for ever. The old man insisted that Calvin should remain in Geneva, to help him with the burden of teaching and looking after the growing number of Protestants in the city.

Calvin wasn't so sure. 'I'm simply a scholar,' he protested. 'What I want to do is read, write and study. I can't be of any real use to you here; you must have scholars enough in Geneva.'

At this, Farel poured out threats and fiery admonitions on the young man, declaring that if he were to ignore the cause of Christ in favour of a scholar's life of study, then he was in danger of judgement from Almighty God.

Calvin shook in his boots at this declaration. He felt as if God himself had reached down to stop him in his tracks. Terrified, John agreed to submit to Farel's demands and so he remained in Geneva to assist the elderly man in the ministry of the church. It was the

John Calvin

year 1536 and despite Calvin's plans for Strasbourg, Geneva now became his home.

There was so much that was unknown and bewildering in this new city. It wasn't just a life of preaching that Calvin had to embark on. He had to begin to get his head around the city of Geneva itself.

John sat down by the fire shaking his head at the memories, as one by one they went through his mind, two years passing by in moments.

Bucer looked at his new acquaintance with some concern. He was pale and wan. The man was definitely tired and in need of some good food and a few nights' rest. 'After that,' Bucer thought, 'we'll soon have him back on his feet. We'll have to watch that he eats properly. I've been warned about how he neglects himself.' Bucer had been warned by some of his friends, how John's health often suffered from lack of sleep and his poor diet. Bucer made a mental note to tell his cook to serve up some nutritious broths and stews over the following days.

'I am sorry for you, John,' Bucer pointed out, as he joined his guest by the fire. 'It must have been very disappointing for you, to leave Geneva. I believe that you only planned to visit the city, but that William managed to persuade you otherwise. He is very good at persuading people, I believe,' Bucer smiled.

John nodded. 'Yes, he is. And so are you. I didn't plan to come to Strasbourg either, until you put the pressure on. But when I think about how things turned out, it's amazing. Two kings went to war, so we had to change our travel plans; that took us to Geneva, right where God intended me to be. I had certainly thought it would be for longer than two years.'

'What was your time like in the city? Did you settle in quite easily?'

'I suppose so. Antoine was with me and Marie. We were a great comfort to each other. Our brother Charles had remained at home in France and we hadn't been in Geneva long, before we heard of his death. He had never settled his differences with the church in Noyon, so remained excommunicated at his death.'

Bucer sighed. He knew what that meant. 'Your brother then was not buried in holy ground?'

'No, he wasn't. Though it means little to me, there is a certain disgrace to where they chose to bury him. His grave is underneath the local gallows ... like a common criminal. It was hard news to hear, but the work at Geneva was just the challenge I required. Before this new life of preaching and looking after God's people, I had simply studied for pure enjoyment. I spent my life flitting around the various seats of learning in Europe. I'm thankful that William Farel put a stop to that. Over time, Geneva has certainly improved from being the immoral city that it once was.'

'That must be due to your influence and Farel's,' Bucer exclaimed.

John Calvin

'Perhaps, but I would say it is the grace of God,' Calvin pointed out. 'Thankfully, before I arrived, Geneva had become far more sympathetic to the Reformed position. William arrived in 1532. And then in May 1536, the city government under Farel's direction, declared itself Protestant. They declared that their desire was to abandon all Masses, images and idols and instead to live under the Word of God. That was when they also introduced free education for the children of the poor.'

Bucer nodded his head enthusiastically. 'That was great news indeed. I rejoiced when I heard of it.'

John nodded. 'Yes, but despite all these good laws and intentions, the city was still in a great deal of confusion. The church was poorly organised. I would say there was some preaching, but nothing else. They needed organisation and good governing.'

'And that must have been why Farel was so keen to keep you there in Geneva,' Bucer declared. 'He saw that you had a gift for preaching and organisation. He knew that you were the right choice to bring the city forward. It is good when the older generation recognises the abilities of the young and encourages them to take over where they started.'

'Well, Farel didn't realise what was going to happen and I didn't either. Eventually, we had to point out to the city council that they were in the wrong and that caused us a lot of trouble ... of course you'll be aware of the system of government they have there?'

Bucer nodded. 'I've heard of the councils, but perhaps you could describe them again for me. I know there are several.'

'You're right, there are,' John explained. 'Geneva is governed by a group of men called the *Little Council,* made up of four mayors, a city treasurer and twenty others. Beneath them is the *Council of Two Hundred*, a body of men elected by the twenty-five men of the Little Council. Any business decisions to be made for the city are first sent to the Little Council and then to the Council of Two Hundred. There is then a further council, which we refer to as the General Council, and this is made up of all the householders in Geneva. There are other councils in the city which wield certain powers and have particular responsibilities, but the real strength is with the Little Council. It is this particular group of twenty-five men who rule the entire city.'

'And I take it,' Bucer interrupted, 'that it was the Little Council who in the end threw you out of the city?'

John nodded. It was hard to think about the city that he'd had such hopes for. But he had to acknowledge that it must have all been part of God's plan. 'I wonder if Geneva is now my past in the way that Noyon is,' Calvin wondered. 'But at least I haven't been banished from Noyon!'

'You haven't really explained what the disagreement was,' Bucer interrupted his new friend's thoughts.

Stretching his feet closer to the fire, Calvin continued. 'It's simple really. At first, things seemed to go well. I wrote three documents while I was there – *The Confession of Faith; A Catechism for the Teaching of Children* and *Articles on the Organisation of the Church and its Worship*. But in the end, the city disagreed with what I wrote about church discipline.

'I believe that the pastor of a congregation should be able to discipline those in his congregation in spiritual matters. However, the city or councils of Geneva have always had that responsibility and were not willing to relinquish it.

'When I declared that unworthy people should not take part in the Lord's Supper, the council again disagreed and declared that the bread and wine should be given to any who wished it.

'Now, I do not agree that people who are living in open rebellious sin, should be allowed to take the Lord's Supper. They are in need of discipline. They need to show repentance, before they can take part in the ceremony. The council, however, became heavy-handed and made decisions about church practice without consulting the pastors. So when Farel and I refused to give the Lord's Supper to those who we considered were living immoral lives, we were ordered to leave the city within three days.'

'I see,' Bucer frowned. 'That must have been a difficult time for you. But what is Geneva's loss is Strasbourg's gain. I knew that you would be a good addition to our people here, ever since the Lausanne Disputation.'

At this Calvin smiled. 'Farel was furious with me at first. He'd taken me to that conference in order to speak, but at first I was as quiet as a mouse.'

'But not for long,' Bucer pointed out. 'That priest Mimard got up and accused the Reformers of ignoring the teachings of the Church Fathers such as Augustine. He said that we were discarding the Church Fathers' belief, that Christ was physically present in the bread and wine at the Lord's Supper. That was when you rose to your feet.'

Bucer chuckled at the memory. 'Without notes you paraphrased the early Fathers' teachings from memory and then you quoted Augustine!' Bucer grinned from ear to ear.

Calvin repeated the quote, 'While this age endures, it is necessary that the Saviour be on high … his body which ascended into heaven is in one place.'

'And then you said,' Bucer added, '"How will you then reconcile the view that the body appears on all the altars, is enclosed in all the little boxes, is every day and at the same time in a hundred places?"'

'I certainly didn't expect what happened next,' Calvin pointed out.

'No indeed. Mimard himself got up and declared that he had "lived in error" and had "spread the wrong teaching". He then asked God's forgiveness and joined the Protestant cause, right there in front of everyone. By the end of that day, the city of Lausanne had voted to become Protestant and, day after day, more Roman Catholic priests declared themselves to be Protestant!'

'Our God is gracious,' Calvin asserted. Yet again, as he stared into the dying embers of the fire, his thoughts went back to the city he had so briefly called his home. Sighing, he pulled himself up from his chair in order to make his way to bed and a much longed-for sleep. 'God was gracious to me in Geneva and he will be gracious to me here. But I had so longed to see Geneva become an orderly, disciplined Christian city. I wanted to see the church there, able to govern itself instead of being dictated to by city magistrates. I have to admit that I am greatly disappointed.'

However, in time, John came to realise that God was behind all events and circumstances. His heavenly Father was in control of all things. He had guided John to Geneva by circumventing two squabbling kings. Perhaps, even now, John's arrival in Strasbourg had some purpose in it. And though it seemed highly unlikely, perhaps Geneva would one day submit itself to the Word of God.

After taking his first service in Strasbourg that September, Calvin believed that he might just feel at home in this new town. 'The people here are very friendly,' he noted. 'There are many refugees, like myself, within its walls. Good Protestants and Reformers have flocked here to find safety from persecution. And the congregation here is so respectful. It is such a relief to be free of the squabbles and bickering of the Geneva church.'

Shaking the hand of yet another grateful church member, as he stood at the chapel door at the end of the Lord's Day service, he breathed a sigh of relief. Strasbourg was going to be a welcome change, despite his disappointment. 'They say I'll have plenty of time for studying, as well as preaching. Getting back into my books, has been something I've really been missing. Yes, I think Strasbourg will be a good place for me to stay.'

But the beginning of Calvin's stay, was first of all marked with tragedy.

'Pierre dead, I can hardly believe it,' he muttered one morning, as he walked out early after another sleepless night. His breath clouded against the frosty morning air, as he wrapped his cloak closer about his neck.

'He is such a loss. I have been left his books, but I will no longer have his conversation which will be sorely missed. The books, however, may prove useful in more ways than one,' John sighed. 'I'll keep the best titles certainly, but there are many titles that I'll be able to do without. These I should sell. I'm certainly not earning as much money as I used to. Even though Strasbourg is an easier place for me to live, my financial situation is far worse.'

John Calvin

However, it hadn't been money worries that had been giving John Calvin sleepless nights and it hadn't been grief over the death of his much loved cousin. The hardest news of all, had been that his good friend Louis had, as John Calvin had feared, returned to the Roman Catholic Church. It was a bitter blow.

'It is a sad start to my time here in Strasbourg,' he admitted, 'but it is becoming home now and for that I am glad.'

In 1539, John decided to become a citizen of Strasbourg. His difficult start was put behind him and he began to enjoy the fellowship and the challenges that the city offered.

One of the friendships he struck up, while he was there, was with a young couple, Jean Stordeur and his wife Idelette. Jean Stordeur had, in fact, come to faith under Calvin's preaching and with his wife and their two young children, attended the church regularly. It was people like these, that made Strasbourg the pleasant, refreshing place that it was. It was the little church there that Calvin loved so much.

Preaching to these people was a joy, as they listened to God's Word and took it to their hearts. He loved to hear them sing the Psalms. Bucer had written a collection of 123 of them, specifically designed for people to sing together. Calvin devised one in French for his own congregation. These Psalms were only to be sung to beautiful, spiritually inspiring tunes – not any old melody from off the street.

Calvin recognised the importance of music in worship. He would often say of it, that it was 'a gift of God' and intended by God to give man pleasure.

'There is hardly anything in the world that can turn or move man's ways in this or that direction in the same way as music. And in fact, we experience that it has a great secret and almost incredible virtue to move hearts in one way or another.'

John's life in Strasbourg also involved working on the revised edition of *The Institutes*. It hadn't taken long for the first printing to run out and so Calvin decided to add in many of the things that he had been annoyed at missing out in the first edition. He now also started working on his commentary on the book of Romans.

But news regularly arrived from Geneva and it wasn't good. Many of Calvin's friends there, wrote that the city was going from bad to worse. Calvin tried to encourage them to continue to follow God's Word.

'Remain loyal to the church of Christ,' he urged. *'We should not be afraid to sacrifice everything as long as the honour of Christ remains unimpaired and we remain true to our service of him. Where strife and dissension reign, there can scarcely be any hope of progress towards betterment.'*

In Need of a Wife

Throughout the early months of his time in Strasbourg, John had his usual church duties to perform, as well as his writing. He had baptisms to take and young Christians to bring on in the faith. The Lord's Supper was celebrated every week. John also had to lead funerals, one of which was the funeral of the young convert Jean Stordeur.

He had not been coming to the church in Strasbourg for that long, before he was struck down with an illness and passed away leaving a young wife and two young children.

John had all these duties to attend to, as he cared for the small group of French Protestants in Strasbourg. They were like a family to him, as he cared for their spiritual needs.

Many of his congregation longed that he would look after his own needs, however. They could see that, since Marie had remained behind in Geneva with her new husband, there was no one who could really look after the Calvin brothers. They certainly couldn't do it themselves.

'That housekeeper is next to useless,' one woman exclaimed to Bucer, as she brushed past him in the

After Darkness Light

aisle. 'I heard the other day, that she lost her temper very badly with Antoine. He was so upset, he stormed out of the house. Next thing, she does the same, so John is left on his own with that unruly son of hers and all those students.'

'What students are you talking about?' Bucer looked puzzled.

'Haven't you heard that John is taking in boarders to make ends meet?'

Bucer grimaced. 'I knew that his financial situation wasn't that good, but I didn't realise that it had reached such a sorry state. We'll have to see if we can arrange it so that Calvin receives a more regular wage. Up till now, he has only been receiving occasional donations here and there.'

'But wouldn't it be an even better idea, to get him a wife?' the well-meaning lady continued. 'You can see by his complexion and sometimes by his lack of energy, that he doesn't eat properly. That young man needs to get married.'

Bucer nodded sternly. It wasn't the first time that kindly Christians had raised the issue of Calvin's health, his diet and his marital state. 'I'm sure you are right,' he would agree emphatically. 'It would be good for young Calvin to get a wife!'

John, surprisingly, wasn't against the idea. He was known for being an awkward old bachelor, even though he was young. Yet, the idea of a wife appealed to him. 'A wife would be a good way to keep my life in order. I'd be able to work more effectively for the church if there were someone to help me at home. Housekeepers are of no use. They have no care for your health or wellbeing. You have to do all you can to make sure they simply sweep the floors. Yes, a good wife would be such a relief.'

John had even preached about marriage from the pulpit and what he thought a good marriage should be. He believed that a husband should be a companion to his wife and that he should love her, that both husband and wife should love each other, putting up with each other's faults and infirmities graciously.

Calvin, in fact, was very forward-thinking for his generation. He criticised those husbands who would stick up for their wives in public, yet at home treated them cruelly and with disdain. Those husbands who treated their wives in such a way, were not just mistreating another human being, but going against God, who had been the one who began the institution of marriage in the first place.

'The reason why Eve was formed out of one of Adam's ribs is that God meant the relationship between man and wife to be as close as that. A child ought to honour his father, for he is his blood, but the bond of marriage is to be closer than that and to be given preference.'

Calvin wrote to Farel about his desire for marriage and even suggested that, when the time came, William Farel should be the one who came to Strasbourg to perform the wedding ceremony. It didn't take long before Farel, Bucer and a crowd of others were eagerly presenting a whole line of suitable potential wives.

Bucer decided to enquire, one day, about the type of woman Calvin was looking for.

Calvin thought solemnly for a few moments, before replying. 'Well, as I said to Farel in a letter: *I am not one of those insane lovers that become captivated by beauty and then decide to kiss all the woman's faults. The only comeliness that attracts me is this – that she be modest, complaisant, unostentatious, thrifty, patient and likely to be careful of my health.*'

As it turned out, Farel had a girl in mind, but for one reason or another Calvin turned her down.

Next, a lady of noble rank was suggested, but Calvin didn't like the fact that she couldn't speak French and was rather snobbish. Nevertheless, great pressure was put on Calvin to proceed and a date for a wedding was set for the 10th of March, 1540. However, by the end of March, the wedding still hadn't taken place and John was busy exclaiming that the only reason he would ever think of marrying 'that woman', was if he completely lost his mind.

So, he was still a bachelor. At least, he was finally given a regular wage of one florin a week. And it wasn't long after, that John Calvin sorted his marital situation out for himself.

In the days and weeks that had surrounded the awful time of plague in the city, John had been called on to help many families who had lost loved ones. He had particularly noticed Idelette de Bure Stordeur and how tirelessly she had cared for her sick and dying husband. She had shown great love and devotion to him and to her two young children, Jacques and Judith. She was in need of a husband and he was in need of a wife ... and besides that, John looked on her very favourably indeed. 'Would she consent, I wonder?' John mused, as he saw her quietly sitting in her pew one Lord's Day morning.

She had a noble strength of character, yet she was also from a poor background – she would not expect great riches and would be more than capable of living on a meagre clergyman's salary.

Two months later, John and Idelette were married. It would be a joyful marriage, but also one with struggles. There would be long separations and periods of illness and pain for them both. Yet, even after all that, John would still write, 'To know joy, to possess joy, to abandon oneself to joy is part of human nature.' His marriage must have given him great comfort and pleasure.

Idelette would always be John's 'best companion' for as long as they remained together on earth. She was 'a faithful help' in his ministry. 'Never has she hindered me in the slightest,' Calvin would eagerly exclaim.

Many in his congregation noticed that the awkward old bachelor, was now a much pleasanter and calmer young man.

After Darkness Light

Yes, they were all very pleased at their young pastor's marriage. 'It was such a good job that we took him in hand,' some would congratulate each other. 'Otherwise that bookworm would never have got a wife …. And what a wife. She grows vegetables and herbs, so that's sorted out his diet. She helps him with his visiting, so she's already reduced his workload. And she does everything with such a loving and peaceable spirit.'

And indeed that was true. Idelette, not only worked hard for her husband, she also put up with Calvin's long absences from home. For the first forty-five months of his marriage, John Calvin was actually away from home for thirty-two of them. He attended conferences and debates. He made friends with men like, Philip Melanchthon, another great Reformer. But he now had someone waiting at home for him and his heart, though always passionate about God's kingdom and Christ's cause, now had a godly and loving wife to look out for – and it was a very great advantage to both his person and his work.

Geneva - Part Two

Letters continued to come from Geneva over the following months. Disagreements were everywhere in the city. Those who supported Farel and Calvin, walked out of the churches and refused to take the Lord's Supper.

Splits were beginning to form in the Genevan church and this worried Calvin. He was against divisions and separations, but it was certain that they did have good reason to complain. Good Christian men continued to be thrown out of Geneva. One that Calvin had been overjoyed to meet with on his arrival there in 1536, had been his old tutor, Mathurin Cordier. When Cordier stood up for Calvin, against the Genevan Council, he too was ordered to leave.

Calvin and Farel finally managed to arrange a peace between the warring Christians. The men who had replaced them, agreed to do their best to strengthen the Christians and to care for the poor. They also agreed to help the school. Calvin was relieved. The very last thing he wanted to see in Geneva, was the reformed Christians splitting into factions. He urged the Genevan congregations to support their new pastors.

'These unchristian divisions are just what the Roman Catholic Church wants to see. Although Geneva is Protestant, its old bishop is waiting for an opportunity to get back in. When Reformed Christians bicker, then the false church begins to hope.'

But Calvin's peaceable reaction to the troubles in Geneva and his support of the replacement pastors, went a long way to improving the relationship he had with his old city.

However, it was political upheaval that helped Calvin most of all. The men who had banished Calvin from Geneva, were now either dead or on the run.

Imagine his surprise then, one morning at the breakfast table, when John Calvin read a letter from Farel, that told him it was his duty to go back to Geneva.

'I left that city with men shouting at me, "Go away, Frenchman, we don't need you." Now they are pleading with me to return! I can hardly believe it to be true,' John gasped.

Idelette looked bemused too. 'A lot must have happened there for all this to come about,' she exclaimed.

'Well, they tell me that after our supporters took the majority in the council, some of the replacement pastors simply resigned their posts. The religious situation in Geneva has become very demanding and they are in need of strong leadership. The council is, apparently, requesting my return, but I'm not sure if

John Calvin

the request comes from the whole council or just my supporters on it.'

'But if they have the majority, as you say, then surely that doesn't matter.'

'No my dear, not really, I still have powerful opponents in Geneva.'

'Well, you've said before how you don't really want to return there.'

'That's certainly true. Who would exchange the peaceful, quiet, useful life of Strasbourg for the fractious struggles of Geneva? Not me.'

'But if that is where God is calling you, Husband,' a quiet Idelette pointed out.

John Calvin sighed. Other letters lay open before him. Even his old tutor, Mathurin Cordier, was urging him to return to Geneva. Was it the right decision for him to make?

John made no decision until after much prayer. Petitions were sent from Geneva, envoys and representatives from the city, travelled to wherever Calvin was in order to plead with him to return. John often found himself in tears as he struggled over his verdict. And after much soul-searching and many sleepless nights he finally came to a judgement.

In a letter to Farel he wrote, *'If I were given the choice, I would do anything rather than yield to you in this matter, but since I remember that I am not my own, I offer my heart as if slain in sacrifice to the Lord.'*

After Darkness Light

Calvin was to return to Geneva. Again he planned that it would only be for a short time. Again he was to be mistaken.

Returning to Geneva had been a difficult choice for him to make. Strasbourg was a place where he could influence France and spend time with other pastors, that he knew and loved. In that city, he had influence over students from many different lands and had made an acquaintance with the leaders of Germany. His time in Strasbourg had been effective and fruitful. Geneva, for that matter, conjured up memories of a different kind: disagreements, struggles and divisions.

However, Geneva could give him even greater influence over France. He would be able to put his model for church government into practice in a whole city, and not just one small congregation.

So in the year 1541, Calvin's time in Strasbourg came to an end and his second stint in Geneva began.

When the time came for Calvin's first sermon in the city, crowds thronged the cathedral in order to hear what they hoped would be a sensational service. Calvin was, after all, the preacher they had thrown out. Everyone wanted to hear him rant and rage at the city that had treated him so shamefully. However, Calvin had different ideas. He continued to preach from the same passage he had been preaching on when he had been banished from the city in 1538.

John Calvin

After the first service, Idelette and John took the opportunity to walk home together – the two youngsters Jacques and Judith walked briskly ahead of them. When they turned the corner at the end of Rue des Chanoines, they could see their house, number 11, not that far away. Calvin smiled warmly. 'It is a good house, my love, is it not?' Calvin asked before he opened the door to their new home.

'It is, Husband,' Idelette replied. 'It is much better housing than we ever had in Strasbourg and the garden is substantial.'

'We are living in a house that used to belong to one of the canons of the cathedral,' Calvin pointed out. 'With the extra allowances of wheat, wine and clothing we've been granted, we should do quite well, I believe.'

'But we still have to be frugal, John. You may be getting 500 florins a year now, instead of just fifty, but there is still a lot that that 500 florins has to purchase. Remember we will be expected to offer accommodation and refreshment to refugees and others passing through Geneva. We will have to be careful.'

'Yes, but it is a far greater wealth than we have ever known. We are certainly no longer living in poverty.'

'And for that I thank the Lord,' Idelette replied solemnly. 'It is a good home for our family, John, with plenty of space for visitors and relatives ... even students if you decide to let them board with you once again. We should be grateful to God for what he has given us.'

'Yes, I never did think to see myself back in this city, preaching the Word of God. I was certain that Geneva was firmly in my past, but now that I am back, I find myself with hopes and plans once again for this great city.'

Idelette removed her shawl and coat before giving them to a servant to put away. 'What plans do you have, John? We haven't spoken much of them and I'd like to know.'

'I want Geneva to be a model Christian community and for that, the church needs a constitution. I would like to see what I began in Strasbourg become a city-wide phenomenon, not just something for a small congregation. The city council has agreed to give me six men to help devise this constitution. If all goes to plan, we will call it *The Ecclesiastical Ordinances*. My plan is for the church to have four different offices:

1. Pastors to preach the gospel and administer the sacraments;
2. Doctors of Theology to train the pastors;
3. Elders to care for the flock and admonish them if they should stray from God's Word and
4. Deacons to attend to the sick and poor.'

Idelette helped her husband remove his cloak before ushering him into the parlour to rest a while.

'That sounds like a good plan, my dear. I have often thought it wrong that pastors should end up doing all the work of the church. It is far too wearying for them and they end up not doing what they should do, which is preach God's Word.'

'Well, in addition to that, the constitution will also ensure that the pastors meet weekly for the study of the Scriptures. Ordinary church members should also be free to attend this meeting. Then, every three months, the pastors are to hold an extra meeting where they will receive guidance and constructive criticism from the other pastors about their conduct and work. In addition to that, there will also be regular meetings of the elders, where they will call individual members to account for wrongdoing. But it is important that these meetings are held with the view to curing the Christian's soul and correcting them in a kindly manner, not strictly.'

Idelette nodded in agreement. 'You mentioned before how you want to start a programme of visiting the sick and prison inmates.'

'Yes, my dear, I have included that in the constitution also. And I've stressed how important it is that a good school and catechism is established. I've expressed how I want the Psalms set to music and that they be actually sung in the church as they were meant to be. And then there is the very important issue of church discipline.'

'Will they agree with you on that? It has caused you problems before.'

'They will have to, but I do wonder, Idelette. You may be right. The issue of discipline could be a thorny one. I suspect that the council will still want to exercise ultimate authority over the church. We shall just have to see what happens. The constitution will eventually have to be passed by the various Genevan committees. I suppose it is then that we will find out if there is going to be any trouble or not. But I assert that *Christ is the head of the church; that the church is the Body of Christ and that every member of the church has his or her place and functions assigned by the Holy Spirit.*'

On November 20th, 1541 the constitution or *Ordonnances* as it was called was passed, but even then it was not without stress and disagreements. It certainly wasn't exactly what Calvin had intended. The council still retained more powers than he had planned. They still refused to have the Lord's Supper celebrated every Sunday. And they still would not withdraw from meddling in church discipline issues. In the end, they only consented to Calvin's plans on the condition that church elders also be members of the council. They obviously hoped to keep the people and the church under the control of the government in that way.

But Calvin never intended Geneva to be under his power directly. He recognised the need for civil government and, although he wasn't keen that the civil government had power over the church, he was willing to compromise. What he wanted was for the city of Geneva to have the best government possible – for both church and state.

The following years would give rise to more troubles and more disagreements. Calvin would always be under attack by someone or other ... and he would always have to work through the problems, being ever careful to retain the church's power and discipline over its own members.

There were many other things that Calvin requested from the Genevan authorities. Some of them were immensely practical.

- *The city should build a separate hospital for contagious diseases.*
- *Refuse should be removed from the streets.*
- *Gutters should be covered and geese, pigs and goats moved to the town outskirts.*
- *Windows should be reinforced with chest-height beams to prevent children from falling out.*

The council willingly complied with most of these suggestions. But Calvin also wanted a good school and catechism to be established. All children were to be sent to religious instruction every Sunday, where every child would be taught that the aim of human life was to know God, to honour, obey and to glorify him.

In addition to religious education, Calvin was keen that children be educated in languages and sciences. So schools for boys and girls were set up.

Furthermore, Calvin set more Psalms to music with the assistance of different music teachers employed directly by the Council of Geneva.

He had a very busy time of it, with all the preaching and lecturing he had to do in the city. But once the council was persuaded to divide the city up into regions, the workload was eased somewhat. It meant that all ministers had their own congregations and particular areas to attend to.

Certainly, during that time, Calvin's work was helped considerably by the fact that his wife Idelette was attending to his home and his physical health. The joys of the marriage were a great advantage, but there were also sorrows. These, however, helped him to identify with others who went through great heartache.

Idelette miscarried once and lost a baby daughter soon after birth. But the hardest grief to bear, was the death of their infant son who died at two weeks of age. Calvin loved children dearly and often spoke of them in the letters he wrote to friends. Whenever he was writing to a family who had little children, he would find some way of mentioning them in the letter. In one, he wrote to a family who were soon expecting a new baby, but there was a little girl, a toddler also at home. Calvin expressed concern that she would feel left out, now that she had to be weaned, but then assured the parents that as soon as

John Calvin

the new baby arrived, the little girl would forget about her troubles in the joy of having a new sibling to play with.

However, John and Idelette were never to have children of their own and Idelette's health never recovered after the birth of their son. John's children would instead be the thousands of Reformers who regularly came to understand the truth of the gospel through his writings and preaching. He would be a father of a spiritual family, instead of a physical one.

He still struggled with the death of his infant son, for in a letter to a friend he wrote, *'The Lord has certainly inflicted a severe and bitter wound in the death of our baby son, but he is himself a Father and knows what is good for his children.'*

During their time in Geneva, Calvin and Idelette entertained many Reformers from around the world, one of which was John Knox from Scotland, who was not afraid of a fight either with words or fists. Knox described Calvin's city in glowing terms. 'Geneva is the most perfect school of Christ that ever was on the earth since the days of the apostles,' he declared.

But it wasn't just the world that came to Calvin, Calvin's teaching went out to the world. The message of the Reformation was spreading across Europe and the globe. Geneva under Calvin's leadership became a crucial centre for missionary activity and evangelism. Refugees from across Europe flocked to Geneva to learn the doctrines of the Reformation, so that they in turn could go back to their countries to spread the gospel. When the Huguenot Admiral Gaspard de Coligny suggested that a group of Protestants should start a colony in Brazil, Calvin passionately agreed. He became the first Reformer to send Protestant missionaries to the New World.

Calvin also made it his business to make theologians of the would-be missionaries and when it came time for them to leave the city, he remained in contact with them as much as possible.

The steady stream of enthusiastic preachers and missionaries coming and going from Geneva, would have incited much interest on the part of believers and unbelievers in the city. Why did these people take such risks? What was it about Calvin's preaching that made them do these incredible things? You really had to listen to Calvin's preaching to understand.

'It is not good enough for us just to have an eye for our own salvation – the knowledge of God must shine throughout the whole world. We do not know who belongs to the number of God's chosen people and who does not. We must feel and wish for all to be saved. Whoever we come across we must aim to make him a sharer of peace ... but it will be for God to make it effective.

'There is no people and no rank in the world that is excluded from salvation; because God wishes that the gospel should be proclaimed to all without exception.

'God desires nothing more than for those who are perishing and rushing toward death to return to the way of safety. This is why the gospel is today proclaimed throughout the world, for God wished to testify to all the ages that he is greatly inclined to pity.'

John Calvin

Under Calvin's influence, not only did Geneva's moral life improve immensely; it became a school of missions, reaching out to a world that few had even dreamt of. The church model, that he began in Geneva, gave the church a true liberty from the intervention of politicians. Many other countries across the world would eventually benefit from these democratic liberties.

But the country to benefit most from Calvin's missionary zeal, was his native land of France. Calvin was influential in smuggling well-trained ministers into that country right under the noses of the French authorities. Soon, the number of Huguenot churches in France was as many as 2,150 with in excess of two million members. Congregations in Bergerac and Montpelier amounted to five thousand people each and in Toulouse, the Reformed church grew to a number of eight thousand plus. At that time, the population of France was about twenty million, so it was a considerable number of Protestants and an important work for Calvin to be involved in.

When France complained directly to the Genevan authorities, about all the Reformers arriving within their borders, the authorities simply turned round and said, 'What Reformers?' Calvin accurately pointed out that he had never sent any preacher to another country, but had simply educated them in Geneva and told them to go and 'exercise their gifts wherever they should go for the advancement of the gospel'.

After Darkness Light

Why then, did such an admirable man inspire such hostility? Idelette, weak from childbirth and illness, expressed her displeasure at her husband's treatment.

'They even write ballads about you and your work, ridiculing you in the streets and taverns. Some even call their dogs by your name.' A silent tear trickled down her face. John wiped it away.

'Idelette, my dear, rest assured that names and songs are of little importance. Just think about what has been achieved since we came here. Children are taught the truth; a university has been set up and the church begins to have good government.

'Yes, we have struggles; some are serious and some are petty. Yet, when I think about my childhood and the lies that I was taught from the priests, I am overjoyed to see a city being brought to the light.

'We were once in darkness, but after that comes light! Translate it into Latin and it should be the motto of Geneva. *"Post Tenebras Lux!"'* Calvin exclaimed.

'Many in Europe flock from persecution to the freedom of worship that this city affords them.'

Idelette smiled gently. 'It is true, Husband; we have much to be thankful for. You are still able to write, preach and work with the church.

'You have completed commentaries on many of the books of the Bible, catechisms, confessions of faith as well as treatises against the Roman Catholic faith. When was it that you wrote that *Admonition against the Relics*?' Idelette asked.

John Calvin

'I believe it was 1543,' he declared. 'I enjoyed writing that.'

Idelette laughed, 'I'm sure you did,' she replied. 'It reads a lot like an inventory that I might make of the items in my kitchen, but instead of knives and forks, it is of the so-called relics belonging to the Roman Catholic Church. Now what was it that you said?'

Calvin cleared his throat, 'With respect to Christ, the relics include his teeth, his hair, his sandals and his blood, the manger that he slept in, the clothes he wore as a baby, the cradle in which his mother laid him, a picture of him when he was twelve years old, a pillar against which he leaned in the temple, the water pots he used during his first miracle, including some of the wine.

'There are five pieces of bread from the feeding of the 5,000, the earth on which he stood when raising Lazarus from the dead and the branch he carried when he rode into Jerusalem. One abbey even claims to have the tail of the ass that he rode on that day. Another monastery says it has the table from the last Passover. A church in Lyons and an Augustinian monastery claim to have the cup used on that occasion. Both Rome and Acqs declare that they have the linen towel that Jesus used to wash the disciples' feet.

'But then there are all the pieces of wood that are reported to have been taken from the cross. If we gathered them all together we would require more than three hundred men to carry them. When you start on the relics of Mary, then it really gets ridiculous.

'Some abbeys even claim to have vials of her milk. In fact, there are so many that even if she had continued to nurse all her life she could scarcely have made the quantity exhibited in our cathedrals and nunneries.

'Six different churches claim to have the finger that John the Baptist used to point his disciples to Christ! And if all the monasteries are to be believed, then each disciple must have had two bodies, several heads, arms, shoulders and feet, just in case they wore out.'

By this time the tired Idelette had some colour back in her cheeks. Calvin was glad. Her health was something he continually worried about these days.

The years passed and as the founders of the Reformation diminished, new ones arose in their place. When Luther died in 1546, Calvin was looked upon as the major leader of the Reformation cause.

In 1549, Idelette also died leaving John Calvin a widower. Close friends recognised that he was a tender-hearted man and would feel the loss keenly.

'I have been bereaved of the best companion of my life, who would have been willing to share with me a life of exile, poverty and even death. While she lived she was the faithful helper of my ministry from which I never received any hindrance.'

Troubles and Trials

Unfortunately, others in Geneva deliberately set out to be a hindrance to the Reformer. It was a time of trouble in Europe. Men in high position in Geneva were accused of adultery. The new King Henri of France continued to attend the burnings of Protestants.

Over the following years, there were the usual disagreements and problems to work out, one of which was a debate with a man named Bolsec. He attended Calvin's Bible Study on Philippians 2:12-13.

'Keep on working with fear and trembling to complete your salvation, for God works in you to make you willing and able to carry out his holy purpose.'

Calvin pointed out, *'As human beings we cannot do good nor want to do good either. There is no goodness in mankind, but God changes man's depraved will through the Holy Spirit. This is what makes it possible for man to do good.'*

While Calvin was still speaking, Bolsec exclaimed loudly, 'It is not true that man is not capable of doing good. If man did not have a free will to choose between good and evil, Paul would not have asked the Philippians to work out their own salvation.'

Calvin replied that Adam and Eve had been the only people who had had a free will to choose between good and evil. *'When they chose to disobey God, however, they forfeited their free will and immediately became slaves of Satan because of their disobedience. From that moment on humanity did not want to do good any more. Instead from that moment on they were only able to hate God and others. God, however, is almighty. He can change the human will and heart completely. God and only God can renew the heart so that the heart may begin to love God and others.'*

During another study a preacher explained John 8:47: 'He who comes from God listens to God's words. You, however, are not from God, and that is why you will not listen.' The discussion was about how obedience to God's words is a gift of God's grace. God gives this gift to his elect only, his elect being the people he has chosen to be saved by his grace.

Bolsec argued that if you believed that then you were claiming that God was the reason people disobeyed and sinned. 'We are saved because we believe in Jesus Christ and not because God has elected us to be saved,' he argued.

Calvin then got up. *'It is true,'* he said, *'that we are saved because we believe in Jesus Christ. We are incapable, however, of loving him, unless God gives us that ability. The belief in Christ as well as the ability to do good comes from outside us; it comes from God. That is what the Bible teaches. We are not saying that God is the author of sin … he is the ultimate example of perfection and goodness.'*

John Calvin

Bolsec immediately started to rage about how the people were being taught false doctrine. The Genevan authorities immediately banished him from the city. But this did not mean that the authorities had changed their mind about Calvin.

'With so much ill feeling about, I don't even feel safe on the streets any more,' Calvin complained one day.

The years of 1552 and 1553 were times of trial for Calvin. In his early forties he wasn't old, but he still wasn't able to stand up to the violent hostility that had surfaced amongst some of the Genevan inhabitants.

Old enemies, who had been banished from the city, had now been allowed to return. Many of them did not like Calvin's reforms and wanted rid of him as quickly as could be. The situation got so bad, that Calvin didn't feel it was safe for him to attend the wedding of a close friend for fear of losing his life.

One morning after the wedding, John was sitting over his papers; a lone letter hung limply from his hand as he sighed a very sorry sigh.

A servant who had been sweeping the fireplace turned round to comfort his master. 'What is the problem, sir?' the old man asked.

'I have many problems,' Calvin grimaced. 'The council will not allow my book on the sovereign election of God to be published.'

'Oh really,' John's servant seemed puzzled. 'I thought you'd preached on that subject already at the

After Darkness Light

Bible studies. Didn't the council banish that man who spoke out against you? Why cause trouble now?'

'Who knows?' John sighed. 'I can never tell what the council will do next. But it is not the book that troubles me, it is these poor students from Lausanne. They left for France in order to preach the gospel of Christ to their countrymen. However, they were betrayed and arrested and are now in danger of execution. I will plead for their release of course, but I doubt if I shall be successful. What I can do is write the young men a letter to encourage their faith.'

Calvin immediately took up a quill and despatched a letter to the suffering prisoners.

'You know in whom you believe, the rock that does not falter or waver. Hold fast on to Jesus Christ. Nothing can separate us from his love.'

Some time later, John heard that the young men had been killed. 'They sang Psalms all the way to their death,' John sighed.

While Calvin's own persecution continued in Geneva, he still found time to write and preach. One of his most important projects was *The Geneva Bible*. It would be published for the first time in 1560 and over the next one hundred years, would be printed over 200 times. It was a project dear to Calvin's heart, as it was an updating of Pierre's original translation. With the help of Theodore Beza, John Knox and Coverdale, margin notes explaining and expounding the biblical text were inserted. The chapters were also divided up into verses, the first Bible to have been published in this manner.

But troubles and trials were never far away and one trouble came in the person of a man named Bonna. He had been refused communion because of adultery. However, he still attended the church services and did all he could do to disrupt Calvin's life and work. He would, along with his friends, abuse Calvin and the other preachers in the street. He would follow them wherever they went, calling out names and singing blasphemous songs as they walked along. In the church they would cough and snort and make rude noises in order to disrupt the preaching. One of Bonna's companions drew disgusting graffiti on the church walls – yet the council decided to ignore his offence. It appeared that divisions had arisen once more in the council and there were those who were for Calvin and those who were against him.

The council again wished to retain control of the discipline of church members. They asked the church leaders to supply a list of all people who had been refused the Lord's Supper. The church would not comply, so the council declared that no church elder was allowed to attend the council. It was unheard of in Genevan history, for any member of the public to be banned from council sessions.

When the persecution continued, Calvin asked the council to let him resign. They refused.

After Darkness Light

'They want me to submit to them,' Calvin grumbled. 'If I resign they're afraid I will head off for Zürich or some place out of reach and preach against them from there. The Libertine faction in the council are determined to make my life a misery, until I give in to them and let them rule me and also the church.'

However, in the months to come, something would happen to stop the Libertines and restore Calvin.

In letters to Reformers across Europe, Calvin made plain the difficulties he was facing in Geneva.

Not only were his enemies out to thwart him, but he was having troubles with old friends too. William Farel had been a man he had respected for many years. Yet Calvin found himself in a position where he had to correct the man severely for his behaviour. It was not an easy thing to do. The relationship between them cooled, as Farel refused to submit to Calvin's direction. The letters between them diminished and very little contact took place after that.

Then men like Gaspard Favre and others resented the direction that Calvin was taking the city of Geneva. They wanted the old pleasures back; the dancing, the frivolities, the immorality. Many who held these opinions, also held office on the council ... and they were determined to harass Calvin.

They thought they'd found an excellent way when a heretic arrived in Geneva. Michael Servetus had escaped from prison in Vienne, where he had been imprisoned for heresy by the Roman Catholics.

John Calvin

His literature was regarded as heretical by Roman Catholics and Protestants alike. So Calvin instructed the council to arrest him when he saw him in his church.

Calvin had had dealings with Servetus in the past, so he knew the mischief this man could do. The council realised that putting Servetus on trial would cause Calvin just as much trouble as letting him go free. So Michael Servetus was put on trial for denying that Jesus Christ was God.

The council perhaps hoped that Calvin might lose this case. If he were defeated, then perhaps he would finally give in to them or leave Geneva in disgrace.

When Servetus realised that the men on the council were in fact Calvin's enemies, he became even more abusive towards John than before.

He would describe Calvin as 'a murderer, a criminal, a wretch without any intelligence, a liar, a ridiculous dwarf' ... and lastly 'barking like a dog.'

To which Calvin replied, *'Insults do not hurt me, but to call me a barking dog is a compliment. A faithful dog barks when his master is attacked, so must I keep quiet when the Name of my Master Jesus Christ is dishonoured?'*

It was bizarre that, in this trial, Calvin became the accused and Servetus the accuser, even though all the churches were agreed that Servetus' heresy was dangerous and needed to be rooted out completely.

Servetus was so confident that the council was behind him, he actually believed that it was Calvin who was on trial and that any day he would be chosen to replace him as minister in Geneva. He even demanded that Calvin be put in prison in his place.

The situation got so bad that the council no longer knew what to do. They wrote to many Protestant cities throughout Europe asking for advice, never thinking that they would all reply condemning Servetus. They could not set him free now, so they condemned Servetus to the stake.

Calvin pleaded for a more merciful punishment of beheading. The council refused. When Calvin visited Servetus in his cell, Michael begged him for forgiveness. Calvin stated, *'I have nothing to forgive you for. You have not offended me. You have offended Jesus Christ by denying his divinity — you must ask him for forgiveness.'*

Servetus refused to listen and would not take back anything he had said or written. He was burnt the next day, when his last words were: 'Have mercy on me, Jesus, Son of the eternal God.'

Calvin recognised that it had been his duty to accuse Servetus of his crimes, to do all he could to bring Servetus to see the error of his ways. When that hadn't been successful, Calvin then had to persuade the council to show some mercy.

'Was it simply because I asked for mercy that it was refused?' Calvin wondered. There was no answer that Calvin could find. The council, as always, were a law unto themselves; there was no telling what they would do next.

A College and a Conclusion

It is no wonder, with all the troubles that Calvin had in Geneva, that he never actively sought to be made a citizen of that city. The council always seemed to be against him in one way or another. However, power often shifts its balance and two years after the burning of Michael Servetus, the Council of Geneva had changed considerably.

The year was 1555 and the February elections had thrown out a lot of Calvin's opponents on the council. His supporters were now in control.

The Libertines tried a brief protest which got out of control and soon they were fleeing for their lives. The long opposition to Calvin's church policies was now over.

'Perhaps now I will be able to set up the first Protestant university,' Calvin exclaimed.

It had long been a cherished dream of his, that Geneva would finally have a university that the Reformed world could be proud of, and after some delays and setbacks it finally became a reality. The building began. John delighted in walking down to watch the stone masons and carpenters busy at their work.

After Darkness Light

'Look,' he pointed upwards, directing Idelette's son's gaze towards a stone mason carving some letters on the door lintel.

Jacques gazed intently and read them out, '*Post Tenebras Lux ... After Darkness Light.*'

'That's right. It is the motto of this city and in some ways the theme of my life,' John explained. 'I remember the dark days of bereavement when my mother died. I was only three years old and it was so hard to picture her face once she had gone. I worried often about whether she was in Purgatory or not. It was a dark, dark time, but then the light came through men like Pierre, my cousin, and books by Martin Luther and others. But it was when God's Word was opened up to me, that the light really broke in and my heart was changed by God's Holy Spirit. This has been what my work in Geneva has all been about and what I hope this college will be about too, bringing the spiritual light to banish the darkness from the hearts and minds of men, women and children.'

And when the time finally came, John had his pick from the best Protestant and Reformed professors in Europe. He asked Mathurin Cordier to come, but he was already committed to another college. But one who did come was Theodore Beza. Many made their way to Geneva when they heard of Calvin's plans for the new university. Students and professors alike wanted to be part of this wonderful new college. On the 5th of June, 1559 it was finally opened and

John Calvin

became a magnet to Reformed students. Within five years, it already had 1,000 students on its roll at the college and over 300 in the academy. Calvin finally had his university to teach languages and sciences, in order that the study of theology could also flourish.

During the year of 1559, Calvin's final edition of *The Institutes* was published, but it was a year that brought him sickness and pain. A bad fever struck him down and then he overstrained his voice during preaching. A violent fit of coughing made him burst a blood vessel in his lungs and he began to bleed. After that was cured, tuberculosis followed, but his physicians found it very hard to stop Calvin from doing anything he had set his heart and mind to.

'I am disappointed to see that he doesn't improve,' the doctor complained one day to Calvin's housekeeper. 'He should not have gone out to preach that day; it was too cold and his voice too weak. Why did he insist on raising it so loudly?'

'He had to be sure that everyone in the congregation could hear him. At least that is what he says.'

'Well, do what you can to keep him warm and out of trouble,' the doctor sighed.

'I'll do my best,' the housekeeper replied, 'but he's due to attend the council tomorrow afternoon to receive free citizenship of the city.'

'Do you mean he has been here all these years and he's not yet a citizen?'

After Darkness Light

The housekeeper laughed, 'Apparently, he thought there were just too many people here who didn't like him, that there was no point in applying for citizenship. Now that they are freely offering it to him, Calvin feels quite touched by their generosity.'

'So there's no point in trying to persuade him to stay in bed tomorrow?' the doctor asked.

'No point at all. If you don't mind,' the housekeeper pleaded, 'I won't even suggest it.'

However, in the months that followed, Calvin's health continued to decline. A nasty bout of tuberculosis plagued him and not for the first time in his life he had to learn about what he had written himself in his *Institutes*.

'In this life adversity will sting us; afflicted with disease we shall groan and long for death; we shall feel the stings of anxiety and sadness when pressed with poverty; ... we shall shed tears through bereavement. But we must think that none of these things happens except by the will and providence of God; moreover, that everything he does is in the most perfect order. Whatever our afflictions, our Heavenly Father consoles us that in the very cross with which he afflicts us, he provides our salvation.'

Throughout these years of struggle with his health, Calvin was still, however, active in directing the Reformed church throughout the world. When Protestant Christians fought back after the dreadful massacre of the Huguenots on St. Bartholomew's Day, Calvin wrote to admonish them for their behaviour.

'You must make reparation for your monstrous, detestable deeds,' he rebuked them.

Calvin's friends and colleagues also needed to reprimand him at times.

'Mr Calvin, at what time did you snuff your candle out last night?' his housekeeper asked one morning.

Calvin couldn't quite remember.

'Well,' she continued, 'It must have been far too late. I saw the beam from under your door when I got up during the middle of the night. You know that you are working yourself far too hard.'

Calvin's usual reply to this sort of rebuke was, 'Would you have the Lord find me idle, when he sends for me?'

And thoughts of heaven occupied his mind considerably, as his health continued to deteriorate. One day, he was lecturing at the academy on Ezekiel. In conclusion he said, *'God's heavenly kingdom is accessible to us at this very moment. He calls us very clearly to come to him in heaven, in the full confidence that we shall enjoy the eternal salvation earned for us by Jesus Christ.'*

Then, one Sunday, the house on Rue des Chanoines was in hushed silence. Calvin had been preaching that morning and the effort had made him so ill they had to carry him home. It was not a good sign. But a couple of days later, he was well enough to dictate a couple of letters while sitting in his bed.

After Darkness Light

The spring months came and then Easter, when he was carried to the church to receive communion. He could no longer preach or dictate letters because of his severe cough. On 25th April, 1564 Calvin wrote his last will and testament.

'First I want to thank God that he has shown so much compassion towards me ... that he pulled me out of the abyss of idolatry in which I was plunged and brought me into the light of the gospel to make me participate in the doctrine of salvation, although I was not worthy of it ... I cherish no other hope for my salvation than God's merciful adoption on which alone my salvation depends. I accept the mercy God shows me through Jesus Christ, on whose atonement for all my sins I completely rely, because his blood cleanses and purifies me, so that I may now stand in his image before his judgement seat ... I have endeavoured in my sermons and in my writings to teach and explain the Word of God purely and faithfully. I have never, in my conflict with the enemies of the gospel made use of cunning and subtlety, but have always defended the truth candidly and sincerely ...'

The time came for friends and colleagues to say their goodbyes to the frail old preacher.

Calvin attempted to encourage them in their faith, but also asked them for their forgiveness of his faults and vices.

'I know these for what they are and they have always made me unhappy. I am a miserable sinner and everything I have done is worth nothing.'

As he pondered what would probably be his last days on earth, he knew for a fact that it was not his works, his Institutes, his preaching that would secure his place in heaven, but the sacrifice of his Lord and Saviour, Jesus Christ.

When he asked permission to visit the council, to speak with them one last time, they would not hear of it, they insisted on coming to his bedside, all twenty-five of them.

His last words to them were solemn. *'I apologise, gentlemen, for this inconvenience and I thank you for the assistance and cooperation I have received from you all in the past. Please forgive me for having done so little, but for often being quick-tempered. However, I trust that God has also forgiven me for these vices and I know that in my preaching here I never once deviated from the Word of God.'*

Still gasping for breath, he spoke once more, *'Always remember that it is God who establishes kingdoms and appoints governments. Therefore always fear God in humility. Trust in his guidance and protection. It is only with the help of God that you will be strong even when your life hangs in the balance. When God makes you prosperous do not become puffed up, but give all honour to God and thank him for it ... When he chastises you and brings you into adversity he wants you to seek help from him, and from him alone. Trust in him who is able to raise the dead. He is the sovereign God, the Lord of all creation. Worship him and give him due honour.'*

'I entrust you all to the care of God,' and with that they all recited a Psalm before they left.

But there was one last letter to write to William Farel. *'I trust that our close friendship will mean as much in heaven as it did on earth. Do not go to any trouble because of me. I can only breathe with difficulty and wait steadily for the moment that I should breathe my last. It is sufficient for me that I live and die in Christ.'*

Farel didn't reply, but instead he visited his friend in Geneva just before he died on Saturday, 27th May, 1564. It was good that the differences and problems between the two Reformers were sorted before Calvin's death.

Calvin's final instructions were that he was to be buried in the common cemetery in Plain-palais. 'There is to be no headstone and no epitaph. Nobody is to revere me after my death.' In fact, although many see Calvin as the cornerstone of the Reformation, he didn't see himself in that way at all. He was just an ember spark in the hands of God, used to light the candle of his Word in a dark and ignorant world.

Now the darkness has gone and after the Darkness – Light!

**For a full list of Trailblazers, please see our website: www.christianfocus.com
All Trailblazers are available as e-books**

Bibliography

Beza, Theodore *The Life of John Calvin*, Back Home Industries, Milwaukie, 1996.

Johnson, E.M. *Man of Geneva: The Story of John Calvin*, Banner of Truth Trust, Edinburgh, 1977.

Kelly, Douglas F. *The Emergence of Liberty in the Modern World: The Influence of Calvin on Five Governments from the 16th through 18th Centuries*, P&R Publishing, New Jersey, 1992.

Packer, J.I. *18 Words*, Christian Focus Publications, Fearn. Revised edition 2007.

Parker, T.H.L. *John Calvin: A full-scale life of the controversial Reformation leader and influential theologian,* Lion Publishing plc, Herts. Revised edition 1987.

Prime, Derek *Bible Answers*, Christian Focus Publications, Fearn. Revised edition 2004.

Reymond, Robert L *John Calvin: His life and influence,* Christian Focus Publications, Fearn, 2004.

van der Walt, Jansie *Calvin and his Times*, Institute for Reformational Studies, Republic of South Africa, 1985.

Walker, Williston *John Calvin: Revolutionary, Theologian, Pastor*, Christian Focus Publications, Fearn. Revised edition 2005.

Wileman, William *John Calvin: His Life, his teaching and his influence*; Robert Banks and Son, London.

Other resources:

Article: *John Calvin on Evangelism and Missions*, Ray van Neste, Founders Ministries http://www.founders.org/journal/fj33/article2.html

Musée Calvin booklet, Noyon.

Calvinistic Theology, An edited version of an address given by George I. Macaskill at a meeting of the Scottish Reformation Society, 1993.

John Calvin Timeline

1509	July 10th - John Calvin born.
	Henry VIII succeeds to the English throne.
1519	Calvins purchase altar of La Gésine.
1521	Calvin receives the tonsure.
1523	Calvin goes to Paris University.
1528	Calvin goes to study law at Orléans.
	Calvin's conversion around this time.
1531	Gérard Calvin dies.
1533	Nicolas Cop and Calvin flee Orléans.
1534	Calvin resigns his chaplaincy.
1535	Calvin arrives in Basel.
1536	First publication of *The Institutes*.
	Calvin visits Italy with Louis du Tillet.
	Calvin sets off for Strasbourg.
	Calvin persuaded to remain in Geneva.
	Henry VIII executes Anne Boleyn.
1537	Charles Calvin dies.
1538	Calvin banished from Geneva.
1539	Calvin becomes a citizen of Strasbourg.
1540	John Calvin marries Idelette de Bure Stordeur.
	Commentary on Romans published.
1541	John Calvin returns to Geneva.
	The Ordonnances published.
1542	John Calvin's son dies.
1546	Martin Luther dies.

1546-48	Commentaries on 1 and 2 Corinthians, Galatians, Ephesians, Philippians, Colossians, 1 and 2 Timothy published.
1547	Henry VIII dies, Edward VI succeeds to the English throne.
1549	Idelette Calvin dies.
1550-51	Commentaries on Thessalonians, James, 1 and 2 Peter, Jude published.
1551	Bolsec debates with Calvin.
1553	Commentaries on Acts, Isaiah and the Gospel of John published. Calvin's opponents gain the majority on the Geneva Council. Michael Servetus executed for heresy. Edward VI dies and Lady Jane Grey succeeds to the English throne. She is beheaded for treason and Queen Mary succeeds her.
1558	Queen Mary dies and Elizabeth I succeeds to the English throne.
1559	Final edition of *The Institutes* published. Geneva Academy opened. Calvin becomes a citizen of Geneva. John Knox ignites the Scottish Rebellion in Perth.
1560	Geneva Bible published.
1561	Mary Stuart returns to Scotland.
1564	Commentary on Joshua published. May 27th, John Calvin dies.

Reformed Theology

When asked to sum up what Reformed theology is, many recite a memory aid called TULIP. At the Synod of Dort in 1618, ninety-three Articles were compiled for ratification. The Arminian group disagreed with Reformed theology on the doctrines of predestination[1] and salvation. There were five points that the Arminians[2] disagreed with and these were referred to as:

T – Total depravity
U – Unconditional election
L – Limited atonement
I – Irresistible grace
P – Perseverance of the Saints

Total Depravity: Every facet of human personality is affected by sin. Humanity is not as totally depraved as it could be because God has a restraining influence, but there is no area of life that has not been affected by sin. Human beings are totally unable to save themselves. We cannot make our own way back to God. It is only God's Holy Spirit working within us that can make human beings repent and turn back to God.

Unconditional election: From all eternity, God chooses a person to salvation regardless of any abilities, worth, merit, or demerit they may have in themselves. A

---

1. Predestination: The belief that before creation, God determined the fate of the universe throughout all of time and space.

2. People who call themselves Arminians got their name from their leader Jacob Hermann. The Latin form of his last name was Arminius. They disagree with Reformed theology on the five points of TULIP.

person does not have to meet any conditions before God chooses them. He chooses them solely because he wants to choose them for his own glory, to show his righteousness and mercy. So no matter who you are or where you are from, God's salvation is offered to you.

Limited atonement: Christ's death on the cross was planned by God from before the beginning of the world. The blood that he shed on the cross was shed to pay for the sins of his people, that is, of those who are chosen by God and who believe in Jesus Christ. Jesus did not die for those who ultimately reject his free offer of grace. The number of those for whom Christ died is an innumerable number. Read Revelation 7:9.

Irresistible or Invincible grace: The Holy Spirit uses the Word of God to bring the spiritually dead to spiritual life, so that they freely believe in Christ. The Holy Spirit can break down any barrier. Nothing and no one can stop the Holy Spirit once he has begun his work to save a sinner. This is what is referred to as saving grace.

Perseverance of the Saints: God keeps his people and protects them, enabling them to persevere in trusting and following Christ until they reach heaven. Every believer has the Holy Spirit living inside them (Read Romans 8:9). It is his presence within us that helps us to persevere and endure even through the worst circumstances.

Thinking Further Topics

1. Midnight Rider
Calvin's mother died when he was very young. How do you think a knowledge of the Bible and a trust in the Lord Jesus Christ helps someone who is bereaved?

2. Memories and Fears
John Calvin was taught lies from a young age. What place did he think people went to after they died? How do we know that this place does not exist?

3. Plans and Playmates
God's Word is without error, but we cannot make that claim for any human being. Why was it wrong then for the pope and priests to have so much control?

4. Tonsure and Travels
In this chapter we see how easy it was to become a 'leader' in the Roman Catholic Church. What did John's father do in order to get enough money to educate his son? Find out what the Bible says a church leader should be like. Read I Timothy 3:1-13.

5. La Marche and Montaigu
Who made plans about Calvin's life? Who wanted him to be successful? Even though one human being seems to make all the decisions for John, God is really in charge

of his life. Read Proverbs 16:9. What does this teach you about your plans? Jeremiah 29:11; Psalm 40:4-6. What does this teach you about God's plans?

6. From Paris to Orléans
Calvin and Pierre are very similar. How is that? But in this chapter they are crucially different. What is the key difference between them? Read Isaiah 64:6. What does this teach us about trying to get to heaven by doing good works?

7. And then there was Light
What was John studying in Orléans? How did this help him understand what justification meant? What does it mean to be justified? Read Romans 5:1. What happens between us and God when we are justified?

8. Reformer on the Run
Calvin's beliefs were against the Roman Catholic Church. If the authorities today were accusing people of being Christians would there be enough evidence to convict you? What about your conversation? Do you love to talk about Jesus with other people?

9. Basel and Books
What everyday object does Calvin describe God's Word as being like? What does God's Word show us about ourselves and about what we need? To find out how he meets our needs read Hebrews 7:26.

10. Geneva – Part One
What were Calvin's plans at the beginning of this chapter? What were God's plans? In the end Calvin was disappointed because his plans were turned upside down once more. How do you feel when things do not go your way? Do you sometimes feel that God isn't listening to you? Why is that assumption wrong?

11. In Need of a Wife
Calvin's friends recognised that he needed a wife. Calvin did too. Are there things that you think you need? Do you ask God for them? Are there differences between needing something and wanting it? What are these differences? When Calvin wanted to choose a wife what did he see as being of little importance? Would you agree with him? Do your friends and neighbours agree with this point of view?

12. Geneva – Part Two
Again John realises that God's plans are not his plans as he is sent back to Geneva. His little boy dies – yet John realises that God as a Father knows what is best. To find out how God is like a father read: Proverbs 3:12; Psalm 103:13; Psalm 68:5 and Luke 15:11-32. Calvin was a keen supporter of missions. He was influential in France and the New World as well as the Netherlands, Poland, Scotland, England and Hungary. Make it your aim to support a missionary endeavour through prayer. If you don't already support one visit

www.wycliffe.org and find out about the triumphs and challenges facing Bible translators in the 20th and 21st centuries.

13. Troubles and Trials
Do we choose to believe in Christ? Is it something good inside us that ensures that we love God? What was it that Calvin taught? Why was Calvin pleased at being called a dog? Do you stick up for Jesus Christ or speak out for him when you hear him criticised and made fun of?

14. A College and a Conclusion
The motto of Geneva was *After the Darkness Light*. How was the church in darkness before the Reformation? If you were to look back over all you have learned about John Calvin in this book, what positive things did his teaching and life bring to the church and to the world? How was his life a good Christian example? Calvin's aim in life was that people should read and understand God's Word. He realised that without Christ, we are in spiritual darkness. To find out how Jesus Christ is the one true spiritual light read the following verses: John 3:19; John 8:12.

Christian Focus Publications publishes books for adults and children under its four main imprints: Christian Focus, CF4K, Mentor and Christian Heritage. Our books reflect our conviction that God's Word is reliable and Jesus is the way to know him, and live for ever with him.

Our children's publication list covers pre-school to early teens. We also publish personal and family devotional titles, biographies and inspirational stories that children will love.

From pre-school board books to teenage apologetics, we have it covered!

Christian Focus Publications Ltd,
Geanies House, Fearn, Ross-shire,
IV20 1TW, Scotland,
United Kingdom.

Find us at our web page:
www.christianfocus.com